THE NORTON SERIES ON
SOCIAL EMOTIONAL LEARNING SOLUTIONS
PATRICIA A. JENNINGS, SERIES EDITOR

SEL at a Distance
Stephanie L. Moore

SEL From the Start
Sara E. Rimm-Kaufmann

*Preventing Bullying in Schools:
A Social and Emotional Learning Approach to Early Intervention*
Catherine P. Bradshaw and Tracy Evian Waasdorp

*Mindfulness in the PreK–5 Classroom:
Helping Students Stress Less and Learn More*
Patricia A. Jennings

*Mindfulness in the Secondary Classroom: A Guide for
Teaching Adolescents*
Patricia C. Broderick

*Assessing Students' Social and Emotional Learning:
A Guide to Meaningful Measurement*
Clark McKown

*SEL Every Day: Integrating Social and Emotional Learning
with Instruction in Secondary Classrooms*
Meena Srinivasan

NORTON BOOKS IN EDUCATION

Advance Acclaim

"During the pandemic, we learned that nothing is more important to success in school than the caring, empathetic relationships that learners build with peers and their teachers. Effective SEL integration is crucial to making that happen. In *SEL at a Distance*, Stephanie Moore shares a wealth of strategies to support SEL in both virtual and onsite student-centered learning environments. When I read this book, I immediately knew that educators would find it essential to meeting the individual social emotional needs of all learners, as well as to making SEL integral to virtual learning."

—Pam Moran, Executive Director, Virginia School Consortium for Learning

"*SEL at a Distance* is a go-to guide for all educators, whether new to online learning or veterans of online learning. Now more than ever, SEL is important to integrate into curriculum and instruction. This book provides clear and practical guidance to do this effectively, and encourages educators to refine or challenge their instructional practices online or in the physical classroom."

—Dr. Anne Jewett, Assistant Professor, School of Education & Human Development at the University of Virginia

"In *SEL at a Distance: Supporting Students Online*, Dr. Moore shares her wealth of teaching and research experience in an approachable text. Descriptions of concepts like alignment, the meaning of active learning, and constructing measurable objectives will help the reader improve all aspects of their teaching, not just in SEL. This book fits nicely into discussions resulting from teaching and learning during the COVID-19 pandemic, but will remain relevant once the pandemic has ended."

—Charles B. Hodges, Ph.D., Professor of Instructional
Technology, Georgia Southern University

SEL at a Distance

SEL at a Distance

Supporting Students Online

STEPHANIE L. MOORE

W. W. NORTON & COMPANY
Independent Publishers Since 1923

This book is intended as a general information resource for teachers and school administrators. It is not a substitute for appropriate training or supervision. Standards of practice and protocol vary in different educational settings and change over time. No technique or recommendation is guaranteed to be effective in all circumstances, and neither the publisher nor the author(s) can guarantee the complete accuracy, efficacy, or appropriateness of any particular recommendation in every respect or in all settings or circumstances.

The author is not a lawyer, and nothing contained in this book should be construed as legal advice. For advice about how to comply with the various privacy requirements that are implicated in online teaching and prepare legally appropriate consent documents, or for any other legal advice or legal questions related to online teaching, please consult your school or district legal counsel or another attorney with relevant expertise.

Any URLs displayed in this book link or refer to websites that existed as of press time. The publisher is not responsible for, and should not be deemed to endorse or recommend, any website other than its own or any app or other content that it did not create. The author, also, is not responsible for any third-party material.

Library of Congress Cataloging-in-Publication Data

Names: Moore, Stephanie L., author.
Title: SEL at a distance : supporting students online / Stephanie L. Moore.
Description: First edition. | New York, N.Y. : W. W. Norton & Company,
2022. | Series: Norton books in education | Includes bibliographical references.
Identifiers: LCCN 2021009005 | ISBN 9781324016571 (paperback) | ISBN 9781324016588 (epub)
Subjects: LCSH: Reflective teaching. | Web-based instruction--Design. |
Emotional intelligence. | Social learning. | Teacher-student relationships.
Classification: LCC LB1025.3 .M6626 2022 | DDC 371.14/4--dc23
LC record available at https://lccn.loc.gov/2021009005

W. W. Norton & Company, Inc., 500 Fifth Avenue, New York, N.Y. 10110
www.wwnorton.com

W. W. Norton & Company Ltd., 15 Carlisle Street, London W1D 3BS

1 2 3 4 5 6 7 8 9 0

For Callie, Jamie, and Justin—you make my heart sing

Contents

From the Series Editor

The Norton Series on Social Emotional Learning Solutions (SEL Solutions Series for short) features compact books for educators focused on recommended SEL practices from experts in the field. Cutting edge research continues to confirm that teaching students social and emotional skills pays off in improved behavior and academic learning in school, and that those skills contribute to students' later success in adulthood. These books are intended to provide school leaders and classroom teachers with SEL tools and strategies that are grounded in research yet highly accessible, so readers can confidently begin using them to transform school culture, improve student behavior, and foster deeper learning.

I am so pleased to introduce this new book by my friend and colleague Stephanie Moore entitled *SEL at a Distance: Supporting Students Online*. When I invited Stephanie to write a book on SEL and online learning, little did we know that education systems were going to be faced with the COVID-19 pandemic and that teachers would be frantically trying to figure out how to teach remotely. This book could not have come at a more critical time; distance and hybrid learning are here to stay. As educational institutions adapted to the pandemic, many realized the benefits of having distance or hybrid learning as an option for a variety of reasons. I believe that this book can become a lifeline for instructors at every level of our educational systems to learn how to teach well at a distance.

I first became familiar with Stephanie's unique expertise in distance learning as a colleague at the University of Virginia, where she worked prior to taking her current position as a professor in the Organization, Information, and Learning Sciences program at the University of New Mexico. At the time she was tasked with supporting those of us who were building our now very successful online graduate programs, and I was working on the SEL emphasis for our Curriculum & Instruction M.Ed., Ed.S., and Ed.D. programs. As I considered how to develop the first course in the series, I was concerned about how to build a supportive learning community at a distance that embodied SEL principles. I recognized that to teach SEL to teachers, we instructors needed to model best practices ourselves. I had created online courses in the past, but they had always seemed two-dimensional and not very interactive. I thought, "how can we create content and learning activities that are not only engaging, but that build the social and emotional competencies we are aiming to promote for teachers and students?" Stephanie jumped at the chance to help me answer this question.

Together we developed ways to make the learning active and engaging: the "generative strategies" she addresses in Chapter 3.

As the COVID-19 pandemic forced educators to learn how to teach online, it became evident that the physical separation of a remote environment was having a serious impact on everyone's well-being. Educators and policy makers recognized that SEL was going to be more necessary than ever as we began to recover and schools tried to return to "normal" operations. This book addresses both of these concerns simultaneously. It provides guidelines for bridging not only the geographical but also the transactional (psychological and communication) distances in synchronous and asynchronous learning, while building the social and emotional competencies to be successful learners in this context.

SEL at a Distance begins with a clear explanation as to why SEL is critical for remote teaching and learning and how to apply the four recommended practices and SEL standards to a distance learning context. The book emphasizes the importance of understanding your individual learners, their ability to self-regulate in a distance learning context, and their access to technologies and family support. The book skillfully applies design principles to distance learning and how to recognize and work with affordances and constraints, bringing greater intentionality to the design process. Stephanie encourages us to focus less on content delivery and more on feedback, support, and interaction to make learning more student-centered. She addresses the importance of assessing and supporting students' development of their self-regulation. This includes self-regulation of learning, motivation and emotions, behavior, learning environment, and interaction with others. She offers useful tips and strategies for building your teaching presence and a supportive learning community through a variety of types of interaction with students and opportunities for engagement. This includes giving students options for interaction such as creating break out rooms with different foci and using asynchronous discussion boards for reflection and processing. The text includes assessment strategies along with a variety of planning tools, making this book a comprehensive but succinct one-stop shop for learning and implementing the strategies needed to support students' social and emotional growth while teaching remotely.

Patricia A. Jennings, M.Ed., Ph.D.
Editor, Norton Series on Social and Emotional Learning Solutions

Acknowledgments

My sincerest thanks to all the wonderful educators I have worked with who have shared their ideas and provided great examples, including some in this book. Educators are the best problem solvers I know, and I appreciate and want to celebrate the creative design thinking and solution framing that I see every day in education. I also wish to thank my editor at Norton, Carol Collins, and the wonderful Norton team that helped to make this a reality. From helpful edits and suggestions to working through how we can distribute useful ideas and tools, I've really enjoyed working with Norton on the production of this book. Finally, I also wish to thank my family for all their support as I disappeared into the void to get this written and out for publication quickly—to Jim, who took on a great deal of the load at home so I could tunnel-vision;

to my parents, who let me hibernate at their place for a while so I could tunnel-vision; and to my three children, who still recognized me and accepted me as mom after I tunnel-visioned. I sincerely hope this book, in some small way, makes your future learning opportunities all the better.

Author's Note

One aspect of distance learning that you need to consider is the potential impact of particular learning management systems, other systems, and tools on your students' privacy, at least if your school or district does not prescribe the use of particular systems and tools and you have to make your own choices about what methods to use.

In this book, you will see occasional references to privacy concerns, but a detailed discussion of the various privacy statutes and problems is beyond this book's scope and purpose. Nevertheless, as if just having to teach online during COVID was not enough of a challenge, you should keep in mind that:

- As you know, there are various federal and state laws that protect students' privacy, even if they are not addressed specifically to "students." The federal laws include the Children's Online Privacy Protection Act ("COPPA") and the Family Educational Rights and Privacy

Act ("FERPA"). State laws include California's Student Online Personal Information Protection Act ("SOPIPA"). The use of some online systems and tools may result in violations of these laws, in ways that are not necessarily obvious. For example:

- Videoconferencing systems that are intended for general public use have very different levels of security, including different protections to ensure that intruders cannot attend private meetings.
- Certain commonly used online tools, even products supposedly designed specifically for students, collect and share personal information about users without their knowledge, and, in many cases, in violation of the Children's Online Privacy Protection Act (COPPA) as well as the Family Educational Rights and Privacy Act (FERPA). Even school-issued computers may carry this risk.

- Some commonly used tools have separate settings or accounts for use in the educational environment. For example, Zoom, which many people use without even thinking about privacy, offers a special education Pre-K–12 account that it says complies with FERPA, COPPA and SOPIPA. See https://zoom.us/docs/en-us/schools-privacy-statement.html. If you open a regular consumer account and don't use the specific education setting, you may put your students' privacy at risk.

- Before you use or offer your students any online tools on your own, check first to see whether privacy concerns have been expressed about that tool. Sites where you may find information on that issue include the U.S. Department of Education (https://studentprivacy .ed.gov/), the Electronic Frontier Foundation (https://www.eff.org /issues/student-privacy), and the Parent Coalition for Student Privacy (https://studentprivacymatters.org). If concerns have been expressed, find out whether those concerns have been resolved, and if they have not, or you are not sure, consult with your school or district counsel.

- Even if you are using a system whose use you are reasonably certain does not jeopardize your students' privacy, keep in mind that:
  - A photo or video of a student, which would include photos and videos of online sessions, may be an "education record" that is subject to FERPA, subject to specific exclusions, if the photo or video is (1) directly related to a student; and (2) maintained by an educational agency or institution or by a party acting for the agency or institution. (https://student-privacy.ed.gov/faq/faqs-photos-and-videos-under-ferpa).
  - A photo or a video of a student studying at home may reveal the student's home environment, which may violate the student's privacy or just make them uncomfortable. Make sure that your students know that they may not take and save screenshots or recordings of online classes or other online school meetings.

- Another aspect of distance learning to consider is whether your online environment will be fully accessible to students with disabilities as required by the Americans with Disabilities Act and, in particular, Section 508 of that statute.

  - Sometimes this is as simple as checking settings or accessibility features in the software or the learning management system ("LMS") to make sure accessibility features are turned on. LMS's and software have accessibility features in compliance with Section 508 requirements. The easiest way to find out more is to search for the software or LMS you are using and the term "accessibility." Microsoft Word and PowerPoint, for example, have an accessibility checker built in with recommendations.

  - Finding accessibility features or information on a product may be much more difficult, especially if the developer has not yet built in robust features. Ideally, a review of accessibility would be incorporated into your district's or state's procurement process. But there are still decisions you can make to ensure or improve accessibility for learners with varying needs or disabilities. While working for the National Center on Low-Incidence Disabilities, I created a tutorial on universal design for learning (UDL) and accessibility for online environments with specific instructional planning and development tips you may find useful. That tutorial is located at http://www.hyperformer.com/UDL_tutorial/.

- Digital Promise, a nonprofit organization authorized by Congress to spur innovation in education to improve the opportunity to learn for all learners, also has an article that may be helpful, "Equity and Accessibility Considerations for Digital Learning." If your school or district wishes to learn more, the Consortium for School Networking (CoSN – www.cosn.org) has a Digital Accessibility Toolkit aimed at supporting educational leaders in planning and decision making.

SEL at a Distance

Why SEL Is Critical for Teaching and Learning Online

First, a bit of history. Tim Berners-Lee created the first website in 1991. The first web browser, Mosaic, appeared in 1993. Maddux (2001) estimated that the world wide web had 50 pages in 1992; by 2000, it had a least one billion pages. By 1996, more messages and documents were sent by email than by postal mail. Google first released its search engine in 1998. The internet developed so quickly that it can seem like we just started using it yesterday while also feeling like it emerged a lifetime ago.

The growth of online learning closely paralleled that of the web, with some of the earliest efforts starting in the 1990s (Moore & Kearsley, 2012; Means et al., 2014). Blackboard launched its first version in 1997, and multiple schools collaborated to create the Interactive Learning Network (an early learning management system, or LMS) that same year. The expansion of online instruction from this point forward was rapid and continues to this day.

However, online learning was not the first form of remote instruction. Prior to online learning, distance education had existed in some form for several decades. Moore & Kearsley (2012) summarize five generations of distance education: correspondence, broadcast radio & television, open universities, teleconferencing, and most recently the internet/web. It is helpful to know a bit of this history in order to understand how and why so much research on online and distance learning already exists. Researchers have been studying and developing effective practices for online learning for more than two decades, and even longer for distance education in general.

Despite these precedents and the rapid growth of the internet, online learning had largely remained a small portion of the K–12 education experience, especially in the United States. We witnessed some expansion of online learning in K–12 during the last decade (Barbour & Reeves, 2009). By 2008, estimates suggested that more than 1 million K–12 students took one or more courses online and that 70% of public schools had one or more students enrolled in a fully online course (Moore & Kearsley, 2012). More recently, the Evergreen Education Group (2020) estimated that as recently as 2018–2019, over 375,000 students were enrolled in online schools across 32 states, and just over one million students took at least one online course through a state virtual school. This growth in online learning—and therefore online teaching—still represented only a small subset of the students and teachers in K–12 education.

That is, until spring 2020. When schools closed because of the COVID-19 pandemic, many teachers who thought they would never teach online suddenly found themselves trying to navigate an instructional environment for which they had little to no preparation. In contrast to preparation for classroom-based teaching, teachers receive no field-based practicum experiences in online environments, and most teacher education programs do not even have a class on online learning for pre-service or in-service teachers (Kennedy & Archambault, 2012). Once they are in the classroom, teachers are often assigned to teach online courses without being given any field experience or preparation (Dawley et al., 2010). This sort of preparation is critical for educators to develop an understanding of theory and practices that facilitate effective instruction in a new environment. Learning how to teach online is a complex process of developing proficiency both with effective strategies as well as with new technologies (Cirillo et al., 2020; Hartshorne et al., 2020; Kier & Clark, 2020).

As if online teaching itself were not a complex enough challenge, educators also worried about how to meet the needs of their learners, now separated by distance, in the middle of a traumatic event. Michael Lyons defines a traumatic experience as "an event that has the potential to overwhelm a person's ability to manage their feelings or emotions and significantly interferences with their day-to-day functioning" (Breen, 2020, para. 6). When students are at a distance, however, it can be difficult to determine which students need additional supports for their social and emotional well-being—and equally difficult to determine how to provide support from a distance. Even students who, at one point, are not exhibiting signs of distress may suddenly experience acute stress or symptoms of an accumulation of stress, for example, if a loved one becomes ill or other stressful situations emerge in or dominate their home lives.

In preparation for the school year that followed the spring 2020 shutdown, the Virginia Department of Education (2020) issued a report discussing the importance of tending to the social-emotional needs students have as a result of the pandemic. They stated, "we know that focusing on social-emotional wellness will be critical to re-engage students, rebuild relationships and school communities, and create equitable learning environments for all students" (2020, p. 101). They included recommendations that each school have dedicated time for the delivery of SEL curriculum and supports as well as for increased training for all teachers and staff on trauma-informed strategies. The emerging consensus seems to be that instead of trying to identify which students need SEL support, we should assume that SEL strategies in online classes will benefit all learners at some point, especially as they cope with an ongoing pandemic that has been very disruptive.

Integrating SEL into online teaching helps to establish a community of support—even if that network of support is geographically distributed—and helps students develop the social and emotional skills they need to manage stress, to achieve their personal and academic goals, and to build healthy relationships with others. But if you are new to online learning, you may be trying to figure out just how to do this in a brand-new environment, perhaps while you are *also* learning about SEL and trauma-informed practices. Change is hard enough when you are adopting one or two new tools or new ideas. It is even more taxing when you are taking on one or more complex changes at the same time. In this book, I aim to provide strategies and examples you can use to translate SEL practices into the online environment. Several of the concepts and strategies I will cover are general practices for effective online instruction, as I want to support you in that change process as well, but most of the examples focus on how to apply SEL practices in your online classes.

As a supplement to this book, I've designed several free handouts to support your work in planning effective SEL supports for online environments. Below is a list of each resource, along with a short description of its purpose. These handouts can be downloaded for free at https://wwnorton.com/rd/moore.

- Job Aid: SEL Planning (Chapter 1)
  - A table for mapping out your lesson or unit plan to align with SEL competencies and practices
- Job Aid: Learner-Instructor Interaction Ideas (Chapter 3)
  - A list of possible practices for achieving a good mix of teacher-student interaction for your course
- Job Aid: Learner-Learner Strategies and Tools (Chapter 3)
  - A list of possible strategies for encouraging student-to-student interaction
- Job Aid: Collaboration & Teamwork Online (Chapter 4)
  - A list of options for planning and facilitating group work, to help build an online community

- Job Aid: Developing Your Course and Your Communication Plan (Chapter 4)
  - Tips for creating a plan and communicating effectively with students
- Job Aid: Delivering Your Class (Chapter 4)
  - Organizational tips for conducting your online course
- Possible Self-Assessment Quiz Items (Chapter 5)
  - A tool for evaluating and reflecting on your online teaching performance

The Positive Effects of SEL

This book is one in a series on social and emotional learning, edited by Patricia Jennings, so you may have already read some of the other books in the collection. The other books include *SEL Every Day* by Meena Srinivasan, *Assessing Students' Social and Emotional Learning* by Clark McKown, *Mindfulness in the PreK–5 Classroom* by Patricia Jennings, and *Mindfulness in the Secondary Classroom* by Patricia Broderick. Rather than providing another extensive review of SEL in this book, I will refer to and build on the work in those books. If you are new to SEL as well as to online teaching and would like to learn more, these books will provide you additional SEL foundational reading and resources. Let's start with a commonly accepted definition of SEL from the Aspen Institute. I've added some emphasis to help you quickly identify the main ideas in their definition:

Social and emotional development comprises *specific skills and competencies* [emphasis added] that people need in order to *set goals, manage behavior, build relationships, and process and remember information* [emphasis added]. These skills and competencies develop in a complex system of contexts, interactions, and relationships, suggesting that organizations must take a comprehensive approach to promoting social and emotional development—addressing adult skills and beliefs; organizational culture, climate, and norms; and routines and structures that guide basic interactions and instruction—and that such approaches are most effective when designed to match the needs and contexts of specific organizations and communities. Put simply, *social and emotional development is not just about the skills* [emphasis added] that students and adults possess and deploy; *it is also about the features of the educational setting itself, including culture and climate* [emphasis added]. (Aspen Institute, 2018, p. 2)

I think it's important to start with a very brief discussion of the research on SEL because—like a lot of topics, including online learning—there are a lot of things being sold and peddled in the name of SEL (as well as online learning) that aren't grounded in research. These things may sound good or make us feel good about what we are doing, but they won't have an actual impact. So, in this book, I will focus on research-grounded practices. Studies on SEL do show promise for a range of benefits for students, teachers, and schools. In a review of 213 school-based SEL programs involving over 270,000 students in kindergarten through high school, Durlak et al.

(2011) found that participants in SEL programs demonstrated significant improvements in social and emotional skills, behaviors and attitude as well as an improvement in academic performance—an 11-percentile-point gain in achievement. Previous studies had documented both the need for supporting students' social and emotional development (Blum & Libbey, 2004; Benson, 2006) as well as the role that schools can play in supporting this development (Association for Supervision and Curriculum Development, 2007; Greenberg et al., 2003). And there are several studies in child development research that document the relationship between social-emotional competencies and school performance, with a clear relationship emerging between increased social-emotional competencies and academic achievement and, conversely, decreased academic and personal achievement associated with lower SEL competencies (Eisenberg, 2006; Guerra & Bradshaw, 2008; Masten & Coatsworth, 1998; Weissberg & Greenberg, 1998). So, we have good emerging evidence that SEL practices can have a positive impact on children's social and emotional development as well as their academic achievement, but it's also clear that these benefits are associated only with the application of certain practices. So, let's get into those practices!

Four Recommended Practices

It's important to note that the research strongly suggests these positive effects result, across the board, when four specific procedures are followed and when SEL strategies and curriculum are implemented effectively. The four procedures are:

1. Sequenced, step-by-step training approach,
2. Active learning strategies,
3. Focused time on skill development, and
4. Explicit learning goals.

These four recommended practices are generally referred to using the acronym SAFE, and Durlak et al. (2011) found in their large study that there were indeed notable differences between SEL implementations that employed all SAFE procedures versus those that used a few or none of them. In that study, Durlak et al. looked at the impact on 6 outcomes and found that when SAFE procedures were implemented, the results were: increased SEL skills, improved attitudes, increased positive social behavior, decreased conduct problems, decreased emotional distress, and increased academic performance. Let's look at each of these procedures in more detail.

Sequenced, Step-by-Step Training Approach

This procedure can sound rather rigid, but all it means is that you use carefully planned instruction to achieve your instructional objectives. In instructional planning, we often talk about *alignment*, which involves carefully aligning content, activities, and assessments to your objectives. Once you identify your objectives (which I'll talk about under #4), you want to carefully map out your content, activities (strategies and methods), and assessments to achieve strong instructional sequencing. *Assessing Students' Social and Emotional Learning*, McKown's book in this series, provides excellent detail around meaningful assessment of student's social and emotional learning. In Chapter 5, I will devote some time to how to meaningfully assess in an online environment. As you are planning your instruction, ask yourself, "Does my instruction align content selection and sequencing with activities and assessments to achieve our SEL and learning objectives?" As I will explain in Chapter 3, having a clear structure and organized class is also essential to effective online learning, so this step-by-step approach to instructional planning is helpful both for online instruction and for SEL instruction.

Active Learning Strategies

As you select your strategies and methods, you'll want to use *active* learning strategies. "Active" doesn't necessarily mean physical movement in this context. There is a difference between passive learning, in which students passively receive information and may be asked to recall it but otherwise are not deeply engaging with the learning, and active learning, in which students actively interact with the facts, concepts, principles, procedures, interpersonal skills, and attitudes we want them to learn (National Research Council, 2000). Passive learning leads to inert knowledge—students may be able to recall terms or definitions or concepts but not be able to act on that information. By contrast, active knowledge means an individual is able to take action on the information they have retained. This information includes not only facts or concepts but also procedures and conditional knowledge, which is knowledge about when, where, and why to use different concepts or procedures. To facilitate active knowledge in our learners, we must "conditionalize" the content (National Research Council, 2000). This means not just presenting the ideas but talking through examples and scenarios, generating rules and decision-making trees together, discussing when one might want to use strategy A and when might one want to use strategy B and when it might be best to use both. In Chapter 3 I'll cover a specific class of strategies called "generative strategies" that specifically facilitate active learning as well as how you can use these strategies in an online environment. As you are planning your instruction, ask yourself, "Am I using active learning strategies that help students understand how, when, where, and why to use the SEL strategies we are learning?"

Focused Time on Skill Development

We cannot assume that students will develop desirable SEL skills and competencies if we do not devote specific time to learning, practicing, and talking about them. As you do your weekly planning, ask yourself, "What is a specific time (or times) I can use this week to focus specifically on SEL skills?" As you identify those times, you can then map out which objectives you want to focus on and then what content, activities, strategies, and assessments you want to use to support that instruction.

Explicit Learning Goals

One hallmark of effective instruction is the use of clearly stated objectives. This is every bit as true for SEL-related objectives as it is for other learning or affective objectives you may have for your students and class. Take time to carefully articulate SEL objectives for your class, and then, circling back to #1 on our list, map out what content, activities, strategies, and assessments you will use to scaffold your learners towards those objectives. As you are planning, ask yourself, "Am I targeting specific SEL skills rather than being too general or vague?"

Table 1.1 summarizes the Five Interdependent Core SEL Competencies developed by the Oakland Unified School District Office of Social Emotional Learning in collaboration with CASEL (Jain et al., 2014), which Srinivasan discusses in more detail in her book in this series, *SEL Every Day*. You could adopt these as SEL objectives or work with a team at your school to adapt them to better suit your context. I will refer to these standards a few times throughout the book, so this table is here for quick reference. But if you or your school are still in the phase of developing or adopting SEL standards, you should reference this section in Srinivasan's book. In the free resources for this book, I have included a tool to help you identify objectives and then align your content, strategies, assessments, time, and technology selections. That tool, "Aligning SAFE Practices for SEL with Strategies and Technology," can help you map out your plan for creating SAFE-aligned SEL instruction.

TABLE 1.1 Five Core SEL Anchor Standards and Learning Standards. Used with permission from Oakland Unified School District Office of Social Emotional Learning.

ANCHOR STANDARD		LEARNING STANDARD
1. Self-Awareness Develop and demonstrate self-awareness skills to: • identify personal, cultural, and linguistic assets; • identify prejudices and biases towards people different from oneself; • understand the connections • between one's emotions, social contexts, and identity; • demonstrate an accurate self-concept based on one's strengths and challenges; and • identify when help is needed and who can provide it.	1	Individual demonstrates an understanding of their emotions.
	1B	Individual demonstrates knowledge of personal strengths, challenges, cultural, linguistic assets, and aspirations.
	1C	Individual demonstrates awareness of personal rights and responsibilities.
	1D	Individual demonstrates an awareness of when help is needed and who can provide it.
2. Self-Management Develop and demonstrate self-management skills to: • regulate one's emotions and behaviors in contexts with people different from oneself; and • motivate oneself to set and achieve goals.	2A	Individual demonstrates the skills to manage and express their emotions, thoughts, impulses, and stresses in constructive ways.
	2B	Individual demonstrates the skills to set, monitor, adapt, achieve, and evaluate goals.

ANCHOR STANDARD	LEARNING STANDARD	
3. Social Awareness Develop and demonstrate social awareness skills to: • establish and maintain healthy interactions and relationships across diverse communities; • embrace diversity and take the perspectives of people different from oneself; and • demonstrate empathy for people similar to and different from oneself.	3A	Individual demonstrates empathy for other people's emotions, perspectives, cultures, languages, and histories.
	3B	Individual contributes productively to their school, workplace, and community.
	3C	Individual demonstrates an awareness
	3D	Individual recognizes leadership capacity in themselves and others.
4. Relationship Skills Develop and demonstrate relationship skills to: • relate to people similar to and different from oneself; • communicate clearly and effectively; and • build, establish, and maintain healthy relationships.	4A	Individual uses a range of communication skills to interact effectively with individuals of diverse backgrounds, abilities, languages, and lifestyles.
	4B	Individual cultivates constructive relationships with individuals of diverse backgrounds, abilities, languages, and lifestyles.
	4C	Individual demonstrates skills to respectfully engage in and resolve interpersonal conflicts in various contexts.

ANCHOR STANDARD	LEARNING STANDARD	
5. Responsible Decision-Making Develop and demonstrate responsible decision-making skills to: • problem-solve effectively while being respectful of people similar to and different from oneself; • behave responsibly in personal, professional, and community contexts; and • make constructive and respectful choices that consider the well-being of self and others.	5A	Individual considers the well-being of self and others when making decisions.
	5B	Individual uses a systematic approach to decision making in a variety of situations.
	5C	Individual applies problem-solving skills to engage responsibly in a variety of situations.

Addressing Some Common Questions About Online Learning

Keeping in mind the SEL competencies, objectives, and procedures delineated in Table 1.1, I will now turn to how to make this happen online. Designing effective online learning environments involves many strategies that are common to developing SEL competencies, so our practices around online teaching can help create an effective online class, generally, as well as help support SEL competencies, specifically . . . if we are explicit in doing so. Time and again, we see reinforcing benefits of effective instructional

practices and effective practices for helping students develop SEL competencies. The rest of this book will be devoted to principles and strategies for
SEL in an online learning environment. Let's start with a general overview
of effective online learning and what the research indicates, specifically
as it applies to SEL instruction. It may be easiest to convey the basics by
addressing some of the questions and reservations most frequently voiced
by educators who are new to the online environment.

IS ONLINE LEARNING LESS EFFECTIVE THAN CLASSROOM-BASED LEARNING?

A commonly expressed concern about online learning is that it isn't as effective as face-to-face (F2F) learning. However, the research doesn't support
this assertion and provides us insights into what matters in online learning. There are hundreds of studies comparing classroom-based instruction
and online learning—so many that we have several meta-analyses of the
research, wherein authors summarize the findings of numerous studies (Bernard et al., 2004; U.S. Department of Education, 2010; Zhao et al., 2005).
You may sometimes hear that study x found this while study y found that,
and meta-analyses endeavor to compare apples to apples. Meta-analyses on
online learning are helpful in clarifying whether one strategy is more effective than another and why the findings are what they are. The meta-analyses
show that neither the classroom nor online is more effective—there is what
is called a "no significant difference phenomenon" (Russell, 2001).

   At first, this may seem surprising, but as I start to unpack it, you will
see that it makes good sense. Clark (1983) summarized findings on edu-

cational technology, showing that it's not the medium that matters, but the design. There is nothing magical about the four walls of a room that ensures a high-quality learning experience, and there is nothing magical about an online environment that ensures a high-quality learning experience. The quality and the effectiveness of each environment depends entirely on what we do *in* and *with* those learning spaces. A classroom learning experience can be every bit as poor or weak as an online learning experience, and you may be able to recall a poor classroom experience. Conversely, an online learning experience can be every bit as effective and dynamic as a classroom learning experience. Most teachers have not had the opportunity to take quality online courses themselves and thus have not had effective online instruction modeled for them (Dawley et al. 2010; Kennedy & Archambault, 2012; Kennedy & Ferdig, 2018). Consequently, you may have a hard time envisioning something you haven't seen before, much less picturing how to do it yourself.

If there's no difference in achievement between a classroom and an online class, what are the differences between effective and ineffective online classes? The same features distinguish effective instruction, whether it's online or in a physical classroom: how carefully the instruction has been planned, how aligned the instruction is to standards, and how organized the lesson is; how effectively the teacher communicates with their learners; what degree of interaction is designed into and facilitated in the learning environment; the different strategies used for instruction; how much sup-port students get throughout the learning process; and other variables. In their book *Learning Online,* Means et al. (2014) identify 33 different variables that show up in the research on online learning! That's a lot, but any experienced classroom instructor knows that we are constantly managing a complex set of variables to achieve desirable outcomes. The 33 variables from online learning research fall into 9 categories: pacing, student–instructor ratio, pedagogy (methods and strategies), the instructor's role and presence, the students' roles and presence, how feedback is integrated and managed, how assessment is implemented, modality (online, F2F, or blended), and synchrony (asynchronous, synchronous, or both). It's important to note that these variables are not all equal. The decisions you make in the first 7 categories have a significant impact, while decisions around modality and synchrony don't have an impact on learning outcomes, although they *do* have a great impact on ease of access to education and on flexibility, some principles from universal design. Flexibility and ease of access become important when effective strategies for SEL are considered.

While the online and in-person learning environments may not be significantly different in terms of learning outcomes, they are qualitatively different environments and experiences. A good way to think about the differences between online and face-to-face education is to consider "affordances": classrooms afford some experiences that online does not, and online education affords some experiences that a classroom does not. For this reason, when you move into an online environment, it's best to design for the environment rather than to try to replicate a classroom environment. The flip side of affordances are constraints, and each of these mediums do have their own constraints as well. As you prepare and design a class, part of what you are doing is trying to maximize the affordances while mitigating the constraints of the environment you are in. At the end of this chapter is a section devoted to affordances that incorporates some universal design principles; keeping affordances in mind is a great starting point for planning and teaching online.

ISN'T ONLINE LEARNING LESS SOCIAL OR MORE ISOLATING?

Another common concern that educators raise about online learning is that it isn't social or that it can be an isolating experience. Learners can indeed experience an increased sense of distance and isolation. Sadly, as remote instruction continues into the spring of 2021, I hear reports of students who feel isolated and very sad about virtual schooling. But as with other findings about online learning, the same sense of distance and isolation can exist in the traditional classroom. Also similar to what is seen in classroom technology practices, the strategies we use and how carefully we plan for interactions—formal, informal, and social—and how consciously we scaffold for community-building are much more impactful than which technologies we select. There is a very large body of research around designing effective instruction online. Chapters 2, 3, 4, and 5 are devoted to exploring research-anchored principles in depth and include numerous, specific tips for practice and examples. In Chapter 2, the importance of self-regulation for successful online learning and strategies for helping learners develop different aspects of self-regulation is explored. In Chapter 3, I will dissect this idea of distance, which is more complex than simply geographic or physical distance; explain "social presence" and how to create it; and share three types of interaction and strategies to facilitate those interactions that decrease the sense of distance and increase a sense of presence. In Chapter 4, how to build an online learning community will be discussed in depth. Online learning can be very social and highly interactive; in fact, the more we plan and design for it to be interactive, the more effective it is, and the more satisfied learners and instructors are with the learning experience. Chapter 5 covers assessment methods and strategies for online education with an emphasis on active learning and on formative assessment that creates opportunities for interaction and feedback.

BUT ISN'T IT TRUE THAT NOT ALL LEARNERS CAN LEARN ONLINE?

Another common concern educators raise about online learning is that not all learners can succeed in an online learning environment. This one does need to be unpacked more carefully, but doing so opens up a lot of opportunities that tie directly to SEL. Research does routinely indicate that some students struggle more than others in online learning environments. In particular, learners who do not self-regulate well struggle more in online learning environments because online learning does put more onus on the student to manage their learning and working environment (Cho & Shen, 2013; Lynch & Dembo, 2004). The most obvious way this shows up is in differences between younger learners, who typically are not yet effective at self-regulation, and older learners, who have had time to mature and develop more skills and strategies, as well as in basic differences in executive function control as the brain develops. Younger learners require more support and scaffolding for regulating their learning process and learning environment than older learners do, and for online learning this will mean that family members or caretakers need to be directly involved in supporting their learning. If you are working with a younger-learner population, for example elementary-age learners, while your school navigates closures during the pandemic or another disruption, you will want to make partnerships with families and caretakers a central part of your strategy. In Chapter 3, I will also talk about the importance of structure in the online class and how you can use that to help provide a lot of scaffolding and support to your learners.

Often self-regulation is treated as determining factor in whether a learner can learn online, but we find that learners are more successful when self-regulation is treated as a learning objective and becomes part of the instruction rather than simply being used as a selection (or exclusion) criterion. Most learners need to learn self-regulation, as do many adult learners, and learning self-regulation is also an important social-emotional knowledge and skill set for learners to develop. In Chapter 2, I will go into detail on different types of self-regulation and strategies for helping learners develop their ability to self-regulate in online learning, with examples of strategies and activities used in online classes.

Knowing Your Learners

In studying how to effectively design learning environments where technology plays some sort of role, the field of instructional design and technology has identified "learner analysis" as a critical first step in an effective design and planning process. Typically, this means understanding learner characteristics like prior knowledge, developmental stage/age, and where students are in their studies. Hodges et al. (2021) elaborated on this more in the post-COVID context of how to think about learner needs during an emergency or crisis. They argue that while we tend to brush over learners' personal and social characteristics during "normal" planning, these become particularly important for effective planning during emergency remote teaching. They note that some learners

> "may have family situations or mental health situations that will greatly impact their abilities to manage learning . . . In times of crisis, learners are under magnified stress, and this will have a significant impact on their ability to focus and to attend learning activities. A crisis will introduce added cognitive and psychological load for learners." (Hodges et al., p. 40)

The questions Hodges et al. raise are good questions to ask anytime you are considering using online learning or some other form of distance education. The following are front-end planning questions (used with permission from Hodges, et al., 2021) that can help you identify needs and anticipate barriers so you can consider them in your decisions, including your technology selection.

RAPID FRONT-END ANALYSIS OF LEARNER
CHARACTERISTICS AND NEEDS

Needs Analysis:

What are the critical instructional needs?

What are critical noninstructional needs (e.g., health, safety, security)?

Learner Analysis:

What important personal and social characteristics do you need to consider?

How many of your learners are food- or housing-insecure?

How many learners will experience accessibility barriers, and what barriers can you anticipate?

What types of stress will your learners be experiencing, and how can you adjust plans and expectations accordingly?

Contextual Analysis:

What major changes in the learning context are occurring?

How many of your learners do and do not have reliable internet, phone/mobile service, or other means of connecting?

How many and which students will have difficulty completing work or operating safely if they have to leave the school or campus?

What assumptions are you making that you can question about your learners living environments to inform your expectations on availability, schedule, willingness to share video, etc.?

Environmental Scan—Infrastructure Analysis:

What infrastructure are you assuming all students will have access to?

What backup systems and infrastructure can you use?

Whom might you partner with to tap into various communication infrastructures?

Content and Task Analysis:

What are the essential objectives?

How can you focus on learning and performance instead of content coverage?

How can you adjust the content to be responsive to the emergency? And are there ways in which you can meaningfully incorporate the emergency itself into the course in a way that helps students manage their stress or concerns?

Social and emotional learning starts when you understand your learners, including the stresses and barriers they face, and translate that understanding into a supportive learning environment. Many of the decisions you make around your instruction communicate, however subtly, your own mindful awareness of, attention to, and responsiveness to the social and emotional needs of your students. By starting with these questions and aiming to know your learners, you may even discover that, because of lack of access to internet and mobile connectivity, online learning may not fully serve the needs of your learners and that a plan that relies on a variety of technologies to bridge the distance may be better. This is a good time to start thinking about online learning as just one option in an array of distance learning solutions rather than the de facto solution, which leads to an important way we can better frame decisions around learning technologies: affordances.

Affordances—A Mindset for How to Think About Online Learning and Learners' Needs

Psychologist James Gibson (1950, 1966) developed the theory of affordances, which is widely used in design disciplines. Affordances are actions or behaviors that a given object or environment or technology affords us, or allows us, to do. Gibson posited that we perceive these affordances immediately, often with little or no cognizance that we are perceiving the opportunity for action and acting upon it. For example, when you arrive at an elevator, the buttons there send you an immediate signal and afford you the opportunity to call for an elevator to take you up or down. The process for perceiving this information and acting on it is immediate, the cognitive process almost imperceptible. Similarly, as you step onto the elevator, you readily perceive your options for where you can go, and you make a selection; and as you exit the elevator and head towards a door, you perceive the handle on the door and the opportunity to open that door—or another door.

In such books as *The Design of Everyday Things* (2013), Donald Norman shifted the focus from only what a user to perceives to what a designer does that introduces either affordances or constraints. Affordances arise from careful consideration, on the part of the designer or the planner, of what behaviors they want to afford. However, this relationship between user and designer is like the relationship between an author and a reader. What an author may intend and what a reader reads are not always the same thing. Similarly with affordances, sometimes we afford things for learners that are actually disruptive or distracting, so designers will also often focus on how they can design artifacts or environments to constrain options as well. Often, we engage in this same process of creating constraints and affordances in our learning environments, sometimes without realizing what we are affording or constraining. Let's explore some of the affordances of online learning so you, as the lead architect of the online learning environment for your students, can more consciously make the most of what online learning can afford.

Online Opportunities

Shifting From Instructor-Centered to Student-Centered Pedagogies: Online (and blended) learning afford you the ability to shift your pedagogical practices so that you spend less of your live or in-person time with your learners as the content delivery vehicle and more time focused on feedback, support, and interaction. We often rely on ourselves to be the primary information delivery channel, by way of lectures. Unfortunately, in the rush to move online during the spring of 2020, many schools tried to replicate live lectures, not realizing this took the least advantage of the online learning environment. Lectures are something you can readily record and let learners watch on their own time. This could be a lecture you provide or an available video you find online and want your students to watch. Rather than taking up precious together-time with learners for this, have them watch it on their own then show up ready to engage in active learning with you. This makes much better use of anytime, anywhere content delivery that the internet is good for and reserves live time (whether in a class or online) with your students for meaningful interactions (covered in Chapter 3).

When the fall 2020 school year started in an online format for many schools and districts, most districts required synchronous time. If you are limited to conveying what you can during synchronous time, you can still create some opportunities for student choice and deeper reflection by how you set up and manage that time. Just like when you provide students opportunities to work in groups or on their own while you float and provide support in your in-person classroom, you can create the same opportunities online. Here is an example Esther Park (2020) shared of how she used Google Meet to create flexibility and openness in her online course (Figure 1.1). She used a Google Slide to create the image you see below, and students could click on each of the "doors" to enter into a different type of space, which were each different Meet links. She then floated between Meet rooms to monitor and support students. You could do the same thing with breakout rooms if you are using a different live meeting tool.

FIGURE 1.1 Creating the metaphor of different, flexible learning spaces to provide students choice. Shared by Esther Park. Used with permission.

Immediacy Versus Reflection and Deep Processing: Often I get asked about whether synchronous (at the same time, but different place) or asynchronous (different time, different place) is better, and the answer is neither because they both afford very different learning opportunities. Synchronous—live video or audio conferencing—has an immediacy to it that you may prefer for certain activities and interactions. It may be useful for quickly quizzing students to see what they understand or to have students do an activity or lab so you can watch the process in real time and provide them with immediate feedback and guidance. There will be times you want to leverage the immediacy of synchronous. But there are other times you will want to leverage the reflection and deep processing that asynchronous activity affords. Used well, asynchronous discussion boards can be a great place within your course to ask students questions that require them to really think about the content they're learning and to synthesize it. Discussion boards that ask students to merely report or repeat what's in a text are not useful, so try to design your questions in such a way that students are generating ideas based on the content, sharing those ideas with each other, and commenting on something interesting. In my own classes, I use the discussion board tool for weekly activities, not just weekly discussions. For example, in one of my classes I have an activity where students create a concept map, share it, then discuss and revise it based on the concept maps other students created. And I give them great flexibility in what they share—could be a visual, a written story, a Prezi presentation, whatever works for them. In several other activities, I have my students work together to generate a resource based on readings. And in other activities, I ask my students to analyze a new example or a new case using the content we've been reading about. In one class, I use discussion boards to present case studies that they must analyze and then generate recommendations. These asynchronous activities can be great for incorporating more active, deeper learning that requires time for reflection and processing.

Providing Students More Time: One of the limitations in a classroom and in synchronous sessions is that they are time-bound. In contrast, both in research and in practice, researchers and educators often see an increase in participation in asynchronous activities, in part because they are not time-bound. In a time-bound situation, you have, for example, one hour, and every learner has to figure out how to participate (or fade back) in that one hour. But in asynchronous learning, learners don't have to compete for a small portion of that hour and as a result can have more equal time to make their voices heard. By unbinding the time element in online learning, you can literally create more time for students. Teachers frequently report that they find more of their students participate in asynchronous online discussions than in live discussions. This is partly because every student gets equal time and space, and some social dynamics that may constrain live discussions are less present in an online class.

Providing Students More Flexibility: And as you unbind time, you also provide your learners more flexibility in their schedules, and many of them may need this flexibility to participate successfully. They may live in a household where there is just one device or a slow internet connection that has to be shared by multiple people, or there may be certain times of the day when they have more access or when someone is there to help them. The flexibility that asynchronous activities affords is one important way you can be responsive to diverse learner needs.

Creative Course Designs—Nonlinear Authentic Activities: Although we often design courses and instruction in a very linear fashion, the online setting is wonderful for designing very different learning experiences. Whether for an entire course or a unit or lesson within a course, online environments afford nonlinear instruction better than the F2F classroom. For example, if you want to create an authentic activity that reflects the complexity and messiness of a real-life problem or setting, you ask students to navigate, or locate, resources using an authentic process. In one class I worked on as part of a team, we used a scaffolded case study design using redacted files from actual cases, using the nature of the internet to create "websites" that students had to visit to gather information. The first case study was very simple—students could locate all the information they needed by visiting a "doctor's website" and the "school's website." And if they read carefully, they would find an email address of a "person" they could contact, which was set up to go to an email account I created with an automatic reply that sent them additional information. The second case study was a bit more complex, with a few additional resources to visit and some missing information (so they had to think about what to do without "perfect" information). The third and final case study had them getting case files that included conflicting doctor's reports, a video interview with a family, hard-to-read scans, and other authentic features and challenges. Part of our objective was not just to give students the information but also to teach them the process of digging for information, thinking about whom they might need to contact, and learning how to cope with less-than-perfect information. Whether by simulations that take students into phenomena or equipment they cannot physically access, virtual environments that offer students the ability to explore a setting in a different place or time, or opportunities for students to work and report from the field (field-based activities), online learning can be leveraged to create learning opportunities that are difficult to accomplish in a physical classroom.

Collaborating and Cocreating: Most of the tools available for online education are specifically designed to afford collaboration and interaction. Tools and environments like Google Docs, Microsoft Teams, and even groups spaces in most LMSs are designed specifically to afford rich collaboration and discussion. Around the year 1999, the web went through a significant shift from being primarily static content posted online to having dynamic, participatory content—often referred to as Web 2.0 or Participatory Web (DiNucci, 1999; Blank & Reisdorf, 2012). Rather than just reading online content, users were now able to interact with the content and collaborate with each other. Around this time, blogs became popular wherein others could comment on the blogs. Wikis became a major source of participatory collaboration, as different communities formed around wikis on a shared interest. Google Docs is really just a form of wiki wherein multiple users can build the content together. There are still a lot of wikis today where users share interests and cocreate resources on everything from a favorite game to gardening, cooking, and other hobbies. These sorts of tools allow users to create a resource together and build that resource over time as they learn and have new insights or tips to share. By using these tools in your online class, you can create a learning environment that is more interactive and collaborative as well as help students develop skills that are common in today's workplace.

Example in Action: Implications of Learner Diversity for Online Learning Decisions

Sadly, in spring 2020 there were reports of schools and districts intentionally ignoring diverse learner needs such as accessibility, and yet accessibility and Universal Design for Learning (UDL) principles provide an ideal way to think about and plan for learner diversity, especially in online environments. Hodges et al. (2021) note that

"rather than discarding UDL and accessibility principles in a time of crisis, these may be among the best planning tools to support learners, including those who might not normally rely on such flexible features. A fundamental premise of UD and UDL is that if a design works well for people with disabilities, it works better for everyone (Fletcher, 2002). More learners will experience more barriers in times of crisis, and designing to intentionally reduce barriers as much as possible will support everyone, not just those with disabilities." (p. 40)

Let's explore a common decision in online learning through the lens of UD: selecting synchronous learning. While it may seem on the surface that synchronous (live) video options can easily replicate the classroom, many have learned from experiences in spring 2020 that educators should not make these assumptions. First, synchronous learning requires reliable high-speed internet access. Many students do not have reliable internet access. If your school or district opts to do synchronous learning, do a survey of how many students have access to the internet in your area and plan accordingly for the percentage of students who will not have access to the internet. If this percentage is high, then synchronous sessions should be optional and should be designed as optional or peripheral instruction.

Similarly, students may not have home learning environments that allow them to participate distraction-free in a synchronous session. If there is one computer or device in the house, for example, and it is shared between family members and is in a communal space, then expecting those students to participate in live sessions without distractions may be a very unreasonable expectation that the student and family cannot practically meet. As you endeavor to help students develop social and emotional learning skills, it is especially important that you practice social and emotional responsiveness to these situations as well. Rather than trying to exert control over their home environments or impose restrictions or rules that could end up penalizing students for environments they cannot control, it is better to pivot to more flexible options.

Applying principles from UDL can be particularly helpful in these cases. You may already be familiar with the principles from CAST for multiple means of engagement, representation, and action and expression (details at www.cast.org; Meyer et al., 2014). What many may not know is that universal design for learning is based on seven general universal design principles that have existed for many years, and these are great guidelines for helping us address the various needs and general variation in the population. The seven general Universal Design principles are as follows (Center for Universal Design, n.d.):

1. **Equitable Use.** The design is useful and marketable to people with diverse abilities. *For example, a website designed so that it is accessible to everyone, including people who are blind, employs this principle.*

2. **Flexibility in Use.** The design accommodates a wide range of individual preferences and abilities. *An example of this in online learning is using a blend of asynchronous and synchronous interactions so learners have some flexibility in when they complete tasks.*

3. **Simple and Intuitive Use.** The design is easy to understand, regardless of the user's experience, knowledge, language skills, or current concentration level. *Setting up your class in an LMS with clear menu items and directions that make it easy for learners to find things quickly and in as few clicks as possible is a good example of this.*

4. **Perceptible Information.** The design communicates necessary information effectively to the user, regardless of ambient conditions or the user's sensory abilities. *An example of this principle being employed is when television programming projected in noisy public areas, such as academic conference exhibits, includes captions. Adding*

closed captioning to your class videos creates accessible conditions that may also benefit learners who are watching and learning in a noisy environment.

5. **Tolerance for Error.** The design minimizes hazards and the adverse consequences of accidental or unintended actions. *An example of a product applying this principle is an educational software program that provides guidance when the user makes an inappropriate selection. In education, tolerance for error (or lack thereof) often shows up more in our class policies and assessment methods. How can you incorporate a higher tolerance for error or mistakes into your policies and methods?*

6. **Low Physical Effort.** The design can be used efficiently and comfortably and with a minimum of fatigue. *Doors that are easy to open by people with a wide variety of physical characteristics demonstrate the application of this principle. Similarly, software that has simple interfaces and features that are easy to perceive and use require low cognitive effort and are more efficient and less frustrating. Establish a clear organization and menu for your online class, and be consistent day-to-day and week-to-week so students can spend more time learning and less time figuring out where things are.*

7. **Size and Space for Approach and Use.** Appropriate size and space are provided for approach, reach, manipulation, and use, regardless of the user's body size, posture, or mobility. *A flexible science lab work area designed for use by students with a wide variety of physical characteristics and abilities is an example of this principle in action. This principle is specific to physical space and thus is less applica-*

ble to online learning, though it may have implications for your learners'
physical learning spaces at home.

I gave you examples of each of these principles in online learning, but
I want to focus on two of them, as opportunities to apply them arise often:
flexibility in use and tolerance for error. One way teachers can plan online
instruction that is more equitable and responsive to diverse learner contexts
and needs is through choosing flexible options that also feature a high tolerance for error. Requiring learners to participate in a live (synchronous)
session has a low degree of flexibility because it requires they be present
at a certain time in a certain space. It also presents low tolerance for error,
such as, in this case, any connectivity issues that may arise before or during
the session. Additional rules for synchronous this time such as dress codes,
whether other people should or should not be present, requirements that
video cameras be on, and other "rules" that have been suggested during the
COVID-19 transition serve to decrease flexibility and increase the rigidity
of the learning environment. These kinds of rules are a good example of the
sort of rigidity that doesn't contribute to learning, engagement, a sense of
community, or satisfaction and that diminish efforts to foster social and emotional learning. In Chapter 3, I will explore how rigidity in an online course
leads to an increased sense of distance and dissatisfaction in online learning.

Instead, consider how you can afford your learners more flexibility and
higher tolerance for error. For example, for anything that's required, use
asynchronous technologies to the greatest extent you can—like recorded
talks, asynchronous discussion boards, Google Docs, and other means of

asynchronous interaction—especially for learner populations who need a high degree of flexibility because of variance in their infrastructures and learning environments. Asynchronous technologies are very flexible in the face of major disruptions, allowing a student to access recordings and participate in discussions at a time that may work much better for them and their other family members. In Chapter 4, I explain how asynchronous is *not* the same as self-paced and can be used for class-paced instruction, so if you're concerned that I am suggesting your class be self-paced, please make sure you read that section. One flexibility strategy is to use asynchronous technologies and interactions for anything that is required of students and offer synchronous technologies and strategies for optional sessions or activities. Synchronous sessions can be recorded. However, if synchronous sessions are required and a student cannot attend, the student will miss out on important learning interactions and engagement in the learning process itself—even if the sessions are recorded. Instead, consider how much learning and interaction you can shift into a modality that is more flexible and will increase students' chances for participation.

Also consider how your classroom policies create either tolerance or intolerance for error. Attendance and assessment policies in particular can be major culprits in creating more error-intolerant, inflexible learning environments. Tolerance for error is a great way to recognize that we are all human and thus both prone to error and trying to function in human systems or human-built systems that aren't perfect either. Especially in times of emergencies, like a pandemic, things are going to go awry. Systems, technologies, and processes aren't going to work the way we are used to. By creating policies and assessments with a high degree of tolerance and flexibility, we can show our students how much we care, how responsive we are to needs and whatever may arise, and that regardless of the physical distance, they are part of a community that cares about them and is there to support them—one that makes affordances for humanity and diversity.

Connections to SEL Teaching Practices

In each chapter in this book, there are a lot of strategies and examples that map directly to SEL teaching practices identified by others. Yoder (2014) identified 10 teaching practices for SEL:

1. Student-Centered Discipline
2. Teacher Language
3. Responsibility and Choice
4. Warmth and Support
5. Cooperative Learning
6. Classroom Discussions
7. Self-Reflection and Self-Assessment
8. Balanced Instruction
9. Academic Press and Expectation
10. Competence Building—Modeling, Practicing, Feedback, Coaching

Here are some ways in which this chapter reflects SEL teaching practices, specifically warmth and support.

Warmth and Support

Knowing your learners and starting with the mindset of affordances are both great ways to plan in a more intentional manner that prioritizes your learners needs and aims to optimize how an online learning environment can support them. In doing this, you can also communicate to your students that you care about their needs and are considering their social and emotional needs as you plan. This is a great way to set the tone, from the start, that your class's online learning community is warm and supportive. Teachers can actively create that support through their decisions by designing environments that reflect flexibility and tolerance for error rather than rigid environments that may erect barriers.

In the remaining chapters I will go into more depth on how educators can employ other SEL teaching practices as identified by Yoder in online classes.

Summary

SEL practices can have a range of positive effects for students, but to realize those effects sound practices must be systematically employed. Specifically, taking a sequenced step-by-step approach, using active learning strategies to support SEL competency development, dedicating focused time to skills development, and articulating explicit learning goals can create a learning environment that supports SEL goals. While there are some challenges in online learning, using SEL practices can help learners both develop SEL competencies and learn how to navigate the online learning space more effectively. In particular, strategies for developing self-regulation are key for learners for both online learning and SEL, and there are a lot of strategies that can be used in the online setting; this is explored more deeply in Chapter 2. Online learning can be effective if educators use sound practices and are intentional in creating an interactive online learning experience.

One important aspect of effective practices in online learning is starting all course design and planning with the learner in mind. When educators know their learners, they can make better decisions about what tools and options best meet their students' needs. The *affordances* mindset is a great way to think about online learning and how to support diverse learner needs in online environments. Using this mindset, you ask yourself, "What do different options or choices afford, and how can I leverage those affordances to create a flexible and adaptable learning environment for students, especially under circumstances when everyone is navigating a lot of complex external stressors that may also change quickly and lead to sudden changes in learning environments and learning infrastructure?" Designing a curriculum while keeping some UD principles in mind—like flexibility and tolerance for error—along with a mindset on affordances creates a fertile ground for online course planning, design, and delivery that demonstrates empathy by being responsive to your learners' needs.

Developing Learners' Self-Regulation Online

In Chapter 1, I talked about self-regulation as an important skill for learners to have to be successful in online environments. In this chapter, I will explore the different types of self-regulation that are important for online learning and the strategies for how you can help your students develop their ability to self-regulate. This is a great example of strategies for effective online learning and strategies for social and emotional learning overlapping significantly and providing opportunities for you to make the most of your online teaching practices.

Self-regulation is a learner's efforts and abilities to intentionally manage their learning process to achieve their learning goals (Zimmerman & Schunk, 2011). Self-regulated learners are learners who "personally initiate and direct their own efforts to acquire knowledge and skill rather than relying on teachers, parents, or other agents of instructions" (Zimmerman,

1989, p. 329). Zimmerman (2002) argues that self-regulation is not an innate personal characteristic, rather it is something learners can improve over time, and so I will focus not just on understanding self-regulation but also on exploring how you can help your learners develop these important lifelong learning skills. There are different aspects to self-regulation, each of which are important to student success in online learning (Cho & Shen, 2013):

- **Intrinsic goal orientation**—a learner is intrinsically motivated to achieve their academic or SEL goals, not just extrinsically motivated (e.g., by a reward)
- **Academic self-efficacy**—self-efficacy is about how much you believe you can do something, so academic self-efficacy involves a learner's own beliefs about how well they can do academically; usually this is specific to a given domain, so a learner may have high self-efficacy for reading but low self-efficacy for math, for example.
- **Metacognitive regulation**—this has to do with how well a learner understands their learning process and can regulate it; for example, this may involve helping learners develop a variety of strategies, choose between strategies, and adapt depending on their needs or the nature of the learning.
- **Effort regulation**—this reflects a student's commitment to managing learning tasks and rewards, in other words, how much effort they are willing to put into it. As you might suspect and doubtlessly observe, learners who are intrinsically motivated and have higher self-efficacy

put forth more effort to manage their learning, thus addressing motivation and self-efficacy can impact effort.

- **Interaction regulation**—this is how well students manage their interactions with others. Given how important interaction is to online learning, as will be demonstrated in Chapter 3, helping learners regulate their interactions with other learners is important to successful online learning.

These different types of self-regulation may sound familiar, like things you help your students with every day in a classroom, and indeed there is a lot of overlap. The difference is that in a classroom, the instructor can manage and mitigate a lot of variables, but when learners are at home or in some other remote setting, they do not have the ability to control their students' learning environments (however much you may be tempted to try). This is partly why it is so important that you build a strong partnership with families and caretakers to support online learning. But research also indicates that teachers can help learners develop self-regulation in the online environment through various strategies. Indeed, a large part of SEL instruction focuses on helping learners develop better skills and strategies for self-regulation; thus by integrating SEL strategies into your online class, you can not only help students manage their stress and navigate their social and emotional development goals more effectively but also provide them an additional form of support for succeeding in an online learning environment.

STRATEGIES FOR SUPPORTING ONLINE
LEARNERS' SELF-REGULATION

1. Partner With Families and Caretakers

Reach out to families to talk with the people who will be supporting your students. Ask them about what they think is important for you to understand about their home environment, such as internet access concerns, the learning environment your students will have at home, and other important contextual details. Codevelop strategies the student can use for regulating their learning environment at home and how you will support your learner together, with clear roles for everyone involved.

2. Create a Structured Class

A "structured" class is one that is well-organized, has a clear schedule and clear expectations, and maintains that schedule consistently. This can greatly help students with effort regulation. Typically, this includes both a weekly routine or rhythm and a daily routine or rhythm. Create a routine that helps learners know what to expect, and manage expectations so they can plan accordingly. A structured class is also one in which the instructor is in consistent communication with students. This takes many forms, like clear directions and guidance as well as individual messages (covered in more depth in Chapter 3).

Online Readiness

Let's explore the idea of "online readiness" as it relates to self-regulation and then delve into strategies for helping online learners develop the five different types of self-regulation. You may have heard about "online readiness surveys" that students complete to determine if they are ready for online learning or not. While these are popular recommendations in public media outlets and may sound helpful in a sales pitch from a vendor, a recent large-scale study of these online readiness surveys found that they do not predict academic performance in online courses and fail to clearly differentiate which variables predict online versus face-to-face outcomes courses (Wladis & Samuels, 2016). Despite there being no evidence that these surveys meaningfully distinguish learner characteristics that predict success in an online format, the claims are nonetheless pervasive about traits these surveys purport to measure, like introversion/extroversion, attitudes about technology, learning strategies, and psychological traits.

There are some interesting findings, though, around personality traits and online learning. You may have heard about the "Big Five" already. These are five psychological traits that have been studied extensively over many years and have proven to be a very stable model for thinking about learner characteristics. The five broad dimensions of personality are extraversion, agreeableness, conscientiousness, openness to experience, and neuroticism.

Of these five traits, conscientiousness is most consistently strongly correlated with academic performance in classroom-based learning (Poropat, 2009; Richardson et al., 2012; Vedel, 2014). Conscientiousness is characterized by planful, goal-oriented behavior and persistence. Conscientious learners tend to be more mindful of others and the context around them and feel a sense of duty towards others. They also tend to be most at ease when they feel organized and aim to keep their life and surroundings organized. The correlation of conscientiousness with academic performance holds true across all levels of education. In trying to understand conscientiousness better, researchers have determined that it is strongly related to self-regulation. Abe (2020) explains that conscientiousness plays a central role in learners' ability to initiate actions, stop from engaging in actions, and direct their attention to tasks and maintain that attention (Abe, 2005; Rothbart, 2007). Abe's (2020) and other researchers' findings also indicate that students who demonstrate a high degree of conscientiousness also tend to exhibit high degrees of motivation and use self-regulatory learning strategies and adaptive coping strategies (Bidjerano & Dai, 2007; Saklofske et al., 2012).

The personality trait of openness to experience is also strongly associated with academic performance, although not as strongly as conscientiousness. Learners who are open to experience seek out intellectually challenging and novel learning opportunities. What's really interesting about openness to experience is that it is the only trait that is negatively correlated with surface learning approaches and positively associated with deep learning approaches. "Thus, openness to experience is likely to be associated with academic performance on tasks involving deeper processing of information and creative synthesis of ideas" (Abe, 2020, p. 2). The other three traits—agreeableness, extraversion, and neuroticism—have weak or inconsistent correlations with online academic performance.

Few studies of the relationships of the Big Five to online learning exist to date. Those that do indicate that conscientiousness and openness to experience are associated with positive perceptions of online learning, but most studies have not looked at academic performance. Instead, most studies have focused more narrowly on locus of control and self-efficacy. This is because the hypothesis was that online learning demands higher levels of self-regulation and self-direction (which was indeed supported by prior research; Gokcearslan & Alper, 2015; Joo et al., 2013; Tsai et al., 2011; Wang & Newlin, 2000; Yukselturk & Bulut, 2007). In 2020, Abe expanded the research to look in part at the relationship of the Big Five traits to online learning." Her findings were consistent with the research on the Big Five in face-to-face learning, that conscientiousness and openness to experience (as well as analytic thinking) were associated with successful online learning.

All of this is to say that learners are not much different in the online environment than they are in the classroom, but the online environment can magnify problems for learners who do not have good strategies for self-regulation. Let's turn now to strategies for supporting online learners with self-regulation.

Strategies for Developing Online Learners' Self-Regulation

Bandura (1989) originally identified three areas for regulation—personal, behavioral, and environmental—but these have been expanded as studies on online learning have continued. Blau et al. (2020) summarize five types of regulation that are important in an online learning environment. Let's use these five types of regulation to identify different strategies that can be helpful in the online class (see Figure 2.1).

Bandura placed great emphasis on giving learners agency in the learn-

FIGURE 2.1 Five Types of Regulation

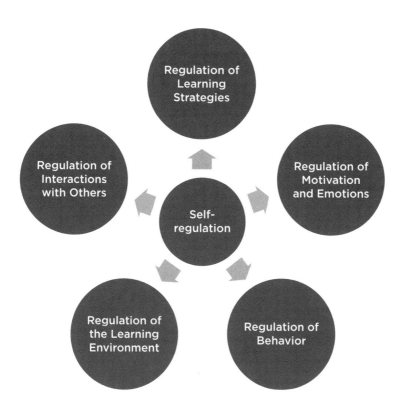

ing process, and this agency can help them learn how to self-evaluate and set strategies. Bandura stated, "in acting as agents over themselves, people monitor their actions and enlist cognitive guides and self-incentives to produce desired personal changes" (Bandura, 1989, p. 1181). Many strategies for developing self-regulation focus on supporting students in exercising their agency. In this section, I will cover both metacognitive strategies and mindfulness strategies. As Broderick (2019) explains, mindfulness is often confused with relaxation, when really mindfulness is a way of paying attention. In this book, mindfulness is defined and explored with Broderick's clarification in mind—the goal is not a "transient pleasant feeling" but rather "a practice of opening mind and heart for greater awareness and attunement to oneself, other people, and aspects of the world" (Broderick, p. 5), and attunement aids in self-regulation.

REGULATION OF LEARNING STRATEGIES—"Choosing and using a variety of cognitive strategies for memorizing, learning, thinking, and problem solving" (Blau et al., 2020, p. 2)

Strategies: Many strategies for metacognition are helpful here—helping learners think about how they learn. Provide learners explicit instruction about learning strategies. Talk with them about what some different strategies are and how they can use them for different types of learning. Have them work in small groups, either in discussions or in a Google Doc, to identify strategies and when they might use them. Then have students write up a personal learning strategy after thinking through when they might apply different approaches. This process helps them develop both a shared and a personal mental model and gives them a great deal of agency in their learning process. When things don't go well, talk with them about what strategies they used and help them identify new strategies or adapt their approach. In Chapter 5, I'll talk about self-assessment more, which helps with all of these self-regulation strategies.

Regulation of Motivation and Emotions—"Regulating beliefs to increase motivation for learning, as well as strategies to control emotions (e.g., anxiety arising from the need for achievement and success)" (Blau et al., 2020, p. 2)

In her book on *Mindfulness in the PreK–5 Classroom*, Jennings (2019) shares a host of wonderful ideas on how to use mindfulness to help students manage their motivation and emotions. Here I'll explore how you can adapt these mindfulness strategies to the online environment to help students manage motivation and emotions.

Strategies: One practice that Jennings shares is the "body scan practice," in which you bring awareness to the sensations throughout your body. On pages 20–23, she provides a guide for this practice. You may find this personally helpful as you navigate the stresses of new practices, new tools, and new challenges. In an online class with your students, you could assign the body scan practice for them to do on their own and report back, or you could devote some time to this activity during a live video session.

Jennings also talks about knowing thyself and managing thyself—creating a greater self-awareness of what our trouble spots are and creating habits for how to manage those spots. You can ask your learners to reflect on things that frustrate them—like when they get interrupted, or when they think something they do isn't "perfect," or when someone says something mean to them. Then you can coach them to think about helpful responses to these trouble spots, both together and individually. You could ask your class to generate examples and ideas together, and you could also ask students to generate ideas on their own and submit a video or a brief writing that would allow you to give them individualized attention and support by way of feedback.

Another mindfulness strategy that Jennings suggests in *Mindfulness in the PreK–5 Classroom* is "calming." Consciously taking slow deep breaths makes us feel calmer. When we practice taking slow, deep breaths, we begin to notice our stress response and calm down. You can integrate this into your daily or weekly routine with your students, dedicating a few minutes to slowing down your breathing together. You can model using this in those moments of frustration with online learning when the technology doesn't work right for some reason, which you know will happen. Instead of modeling a stress-filled response, you can model taking a deep breath, calming down, and then working through the problem. Jennings provides all kinds of variations on this strategy in her book, and they can be readily adapted to online classes by either giving students the activity to do on their own or doing them during your live class sessions. For example, during one of your live video conferencing sessions you could do an activity involving shaking up a jar of water and glitter, or having them fill a jar with water and glitter (with help from a caretaker!) and shake it, then asking students to generate words that describe that feeling. You could ask the students to write a story or poem and submit it to you online throught your school's LMS (e.g., Desire2Learn or Canvas). For young learners, you can encourage them to bring a "breathing buddy" (Jennings, 2019, p. 47)—a stuffed toy, a beanbag, a rock, or whatever the child chooses—to learn with them and take time to breathe with their buddies every day.

REGULATION OF BEHAVIOR—Selecting actions that help control behavior, such as setting aside time to complete tasks and meet deadlines or using/designing learning strategies that help one achieve their learning goals (Blau et al., 2020)

Strategies: Set aside some time in class to talk with students about how they can plan for tasks and deadlines that are part of the class. Be sure you work with them to generate ideas that will work for them. This helps ensure their plan is actually feasible for them and helps them develop planning skills rather than you planning for them. Work with students to map out the tasks and deadlines, model how you would estimate time, help them identify other activities they should anticipate as they plan, give some examples of how they could plan time, then ask them to generate their personal plans for completing work. They could share this in small groups, as a class, or just with you. One great activity that Teomara Rutherford (2020) shared online made use of Padlet for this sort of activity (Figure 2.2). In the activity, she

FIGURE 2.2 Example activity for behavior regulation using Padlet. Adapted from an activity used in the course of Dr. Teomara Rutherford at University of Delaware. Used with permission.

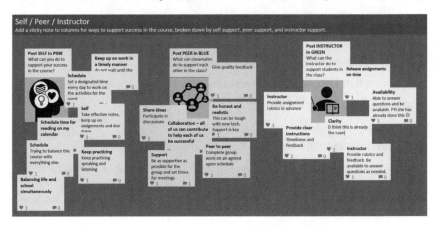

has her students brainstorm ways they can support success in their online class, broken down into self support, peer support, and instructor support.

REGULATION OF THE LEARNING ENVIRONMENT—

"An effort to build an environment that will facilitate the completion of learning tasks" (Blau et al., 2020, p. 2)

Strategies: Specific strategies for regulating the learning environment include structuring the learning environment to support learning, seeking information, reviewing, and seeking assistance. "Self-regulated learners know how to seek or extract the resources, help, or information they need from their learning environments in order to achieve their learning goals" (Delen & Liew, 2016). Educators can help learners develop these strategies through explicit instruction and talking about strategies for regulating the environment, followed by active learning strategies in which students generate ideas for how they can regulate their environments, identify potential problem spaces, and brainstorm solutions (with each other, with you, and/or with a caretaker). For example, ask students to describe their learning environment: what do they have around them that is helpful? A great example of an activity in Padlet wherein students learn how to regulate their learning environments appears in Figure 2.3, which is from LaToya Sapp. What do the students have around them that could be distracting? Who can they ask for help or support if they run into different types of issues? This activity can enrich your understanding of your learners' contexts so that your instruction and decision-making are better informed, and it can illuminate some opportunities for working with learners to exercise some agency. For younger learners, this will involve working with their families or caretakers, but even young learners can be given a great deal of agency in thinking through how they can set up a supportive learning environment.

Jennings (2019) describes one particularly good mindfulness strategy in *Mindfulness in the PreK–5 Classroom* that you can use with your learners to help them learn how to regulate their learning environment: focusing. You may have heard the rule of 7±2—that we can only attend to that many things at one time, but it turns out our short-term memory span is in fact smaller than that. Cowan (2001, 2010) explains that our capacity is really 4±1. This means that we humans, even adults, have a very limited capacity for what we can pay attention to—and we can be very distractible. Right

FIGURE 2.3 Example of learner environment-regulation activity using Padlet. Shared by LaToya Sapp, a gifted and talented specialist at Northside Independent School District in San Antonio, TX. Used with permission.

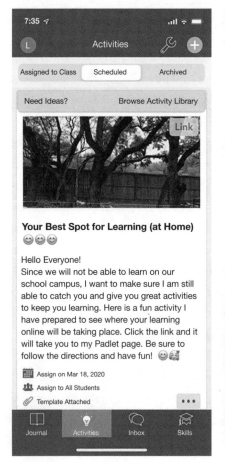
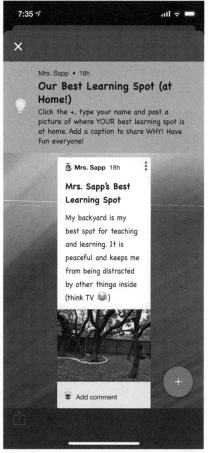

now, as you read this, you're probably also closely listening for other sounds in your home, alerts from your computer or phone, noticing if a pet moves or does something, tuning other family members in or out, thinking about an interaction you had with a parent last week, thinking about a news item you just read, and so on. Focusing is a practice that helps us sustain our attention on what is important. For this practice, you will need a chime or a bell. (Jennings provides more detailed guidance in her book for this activity.) In an online class, you could easily do this activity during a live session with your students. You could also record a video of yourself guiding your students through this activity and have them watch it and complete it on their own, then submit a quick open-ended self-assessment at the end through the Assignment or a quiz tool in your LMS to verify they completed the activity and to help them develop self-assessment skills.

If you detect that some of your students are struggling with sleep or stress, you could recording a video of yourself guiding students through the Sleep and Stress Response activities that Jennings explores in Chapter 4 of *Mindfulness in the PreK–5 Classroom*. This may be particularly helpful for students who are feeling great stress and anxiety during remote learning either because they miss their friends or because a family member is ill or some other stressful thing is happening in their home environment. By recording sleep and stress response activities for your students, you can provide your learners the flexibility to watch them when they can help with sleep or stress. You could make them available every week to students as a recurring weekly feature and support. If you want to check in with your students, you could incorporate weekly check-ins that include these sleep and stress response activities, to which they submit a report on how well they are sleeping, what their stress level is, and how they are doing. Broderick's (2019) book in this series, *Mindfulness in the Secondary Classroom*, has an entire chapter dedicated to stress and how mindfulness can help. You may find that adapting some of the activities in that chapter into activities you already do with your students may be beneficial, especially as we continue to navigate an extended, stressful social period. For some of these activities, you could devote time during your live sessions to walk students through an exercise, for other activities you could create them as weekly activities your students complete on their own time and submit by the end of the week or bring back and share during live class time. For anything that may be too sensitive or private to share in front of others, have your students use a blog tool for journaling or a voice or video recording tool (or let them pick a tool so they can exercise agency and do so in a way that feels natural and safe for them) to submit their responses.

REGULATION OF INTERACTIONS WITH OTHERS—As I will demonstrate, interactions are critical to effective online instruction; however, "the challenge of self-regulation also arises during online interactions and collaborative processes in virtual teams" (Blau et al., 2020, p. 2).

This is very similar to what Jennings (2019) refers to as the "eighth sense"—the "relational sense" that "allows us to tune in to others" (p. 14). You can facilitate even young learners development of this "eighth sense" by helping them begin to notice and describe what they are feeling as they interact with others.

Strategies: Using synchronous active learning activities (not synchronous *lecturing*), wherein students are engaged in activities that require they interact with each other, collaborate, and work in teams, can help with motivation and achievement, but this also means students need to have or to develop skills for regulating their interactions with others. Jennings talks about helping learners develop mindful listening skills in the classroom, which supports relationship skills.

One way this is often done online, again giving learners agency, is to ask the class to generate guidelines or rules for engagement that the class adopts and shares. You can also lead the class in identifying specific roles and responsibilities so there are clear parameters for cooperation. Guide teams through a process of mapping out a team plan for how they will produce their outcomes together by meeting with your students in small online groups instead of as a whole class. You can use features like breakout rooms to put students into groups then spend 10 minutes or so with each group helping them with their plan while the other groups work on other tasks.

Jennings (2019) also provides excellent mindfulness strategies for cultivating kindness and compassion that can be readily implemented in an online class. Mindful Listening, in particular, is an excellent strategy for learning to regulate interactions with others as well as other areas of self-regulation. One activity Jennings describes is putting students in pairs and having them read a poem or short story to each other. In an online environment, you can do this using breakout rooms in live video conferencing software such as Zoom, Collaborate, and other live collaboration tools. If you have small group collaborations in your class, you could adapt this activity so that that you break your class out into their small groups, and each group starts with a mindful listening period in which each group member shares their ideas or thoughts on the project, then they take a few minutes to answer questions to help them generate awareness of their mindfulness, and then the group begins to work on their project together.

If you are interested in incorporating more mindfulness strategies into your practices, Jennings's *Mindfulness in the PreK–5 Classroom* and Broderick's *Mindfulness in the Secondary Classroom: A Guide for Teaching Adolescents* introduce research-anchored practices.

Digital Literacy and Self-Regulation

One additional aspect of self-regulation in an online or digital environment is developing skills for navigating and coping with an information-rich environment that can be dense in multimedia and hypermedia and that presents many open-ended features. While these qualities can be very beneficial to the learning process, they also can be distracting or confusing. Not only can students get distracted by items or features in their physical environments, but they can also get distracted or confused in the digital environment itself. You may have heard someone say that younger generations of learners already know how to navigate these digital environments, but research doesn't support the assertion that younger learners are already adept at navigating information-rich environments, especially digital learning environments. Research on generational differences finds that no real differences exist between the generations (Oh & Reeves, 2014; Quinn, 2018), plus we also find that learner "preferences" don't necessarily lead to good decisions or choices around what to focus on (Kirschner & van Merriënboer, 2013). Instead, we find that navigating online or digital environments is a *lot* like learning to read. Any person, regardless of age, needs to become literate in the information environment they're trying to navigate. Thus, part of our task becomes helping our learners develop *digital* literacy.

According to Ng (2012), distance learning requires a variety of cognitive, social, emotional, and technological skills. Researchers in distance and online learning have long posited that to learn effectively in digital environments, learners must develop a set of skills generally referred to as "digital literacy" (Eshet-Alkalai & Soffer, 2012; Ferrari, 2012; Porat et al., 2018; Alexander et al., 2019; Adams Becker et al., 2017). While there are several different models commonly used to discuss digital literacy, they all include social and emotional skills as part of their digital literacy framework. So, as you help your learners develop skills necessary for learning in an online environment, you can also simultaneously support SEL goals and outcomes. Much of this should sound familiar. In discussing self-regulation, we covered cognitive and metacognitive, motivation and emotions, and social self-regulation. We have also discussed managing the learning environment. Digital literacy is an extension of all of these, particularly of managing the learning environment.

At the core of this is the idea of attention—learning how to pay attention and what to pay attention to. We have already covered some foundational ideas and strategies for training attention, such as breathing awareness, calming, and focusing. Building these activities your class routines to help your learners focus their attention can help them navigate distracting environments and information-dense environments. Additionally, there are ways you can help your learners process the complex environment within your online class itself and pay attention to what is salient (Schlatter & Levinson, 2013). Once you have your class ready to go, create a Class Tour video wherein you walk your students through the class—show them (and/or their caretakers) how your online class is set up, what to pay attention to when, and even provide them with a handout that summarizes the class schedule. During the first week of class, devote time to orienting your students and give them opportunities to practice using the tools and features in a low- or no-stakes manner. This can significantly reduce their "cognitive load" as they try to make sense of all the information (Oviatt, 2006). You could have activities like a scavenger hunt or start with an activity that involves talking about learning environments and generating ideas together on how to manage learning at home and how to manage the online environment.

Additionally, you can use visual and auditory cues in your online class to help learners focus on what is most salient. One of my favorite resources for visual design principles that anyone can apply is Robin Williams's *The Non-Designers Design Book*. You can help a learner attend to information, ignore information, and organization information cognitively by using design principles she discusses in her book. For example, principles such as contrast, repetition, alignment, and proximity can help your learners cognitively organize and integrate the information you present. Using font color and size to help create contrast and draw attention can also help learners better organize and integrate the content. You can apply these design principles both to your learning materials (handouts, videos, PowerPoints, etc.) as well as to your course interface and the layout in your LMS. Another excellent resource is Mayer's *Multimedia Learning* text. You can easily search this book to find research-anchored principles for designing instructional materials based on how humans process visual and auditory information. These principles are also summarized in *e-Learning and the Science of Instruction*. One or the other of these texts would be a good resource to have on hand, although the *Multimedia Learning* text is more of a summary of the research process and the principles, whereas *e-Learning and the Science of Instruction* is more focused on application of the principles. This reading may take some time, and you likely will not be able to fully addressed all of the ideas or principles your first time through teaching an online course, but you can work on applying these principles over several iterations of your course. Typically, the materials you create as you apply these principles are materials you can immediately cycle into use in your classroom, so there is a good return on your time investment. Be patient with yourself and your process, and spread out your continual improvement and revisions over time. I usually give myself about three iterations of an online course to get everything the way I want it.

Connections to SEL Teaching Practices

In this chapter I've touched on two of the teaching practices for SEL that Yoder (2014) identified for online teaching: student-centered discipline and teacher language.

Student-Centered Discipline

Classroom management strategies should support students in being self-directive and having some say in what happens in the classroom. Many of the strategies I have discussed thus far can help with online classroom management, such as establishing routines, setting course rules and expectations, and integrating mindfulness practices. In Chapters 3 and 4, I will share even more strategies, such as providing multiple communication channels for different types of interactions and creating a community of support.

Teacher Language

Encourage students to monitor and regulate their own behavior, do not just tell them how to behave. For example, Yoder (2014) suggests asking students what strategies they have learned to apply when they come across a problem that they are not sure how to solve. There is nothing about an online environment that should prohibit you from adopting more supportive language, which can also be helpful in addressing self-regulation, as discussed in this chapter.

Summary

While there are some challenges in online learning, using SEL practices can help learners both develop SEL competencies and learn how to navigate the online learning space more effectively. Strategies for developing self-regulation are key for learners both for online learning and for SEL, and there are a lot of strategies that educators can use in the online setting. Rather than thinking of "online readiness" as a trait that learners either have or do not have, it is more beneficial to students to help them develop strategies they can use to manage their learning processes. Specifically, educators can help learners develop five different types of self-regulation: regulation of their learning strategies, regulation of their motivation and emotions, regulation of their behavior, regulation of their learning environments, and regulation of their interactions with others. By making self-regulation an explicit objective and integrating activities to support learners, educators can help them develop skills that serve them well not just in online classes but throughout their learning and on into adulthood.

Helping learners navigate information-dense online environments also means helping them develop their digital literacy. You can do this in part by designing an online environment that facilitates clear organization and communication, such as by employing good visual design principles that help learners organize and chunk information. But you can also explicitly teach learners how to navigate digital environments. In fact, all models of digital literacy include social and emotional skills as part of their frameworks.

Helping learners develop their skills in knowing what to pay attention to and how to tune out distracting information supports both SEL and digital literacy. By designing routines and activities that help your learners cultivate awareness and use calming and focusing techniques, you can simultaneously help them with navigating the online environment and developing their social and emotional competencies.

Bridging Distance Through Presence and Interaction

One of the most common questions or concerns about online learning is whether it can be interactive and social. Not only can it be, but research shows that learning and satisfaction increase as the level of interaction in online courses increases. In this chapter, I will dissect what is meant by "distance" and explore the idea of "social presence"—two general ideas that teachers can use to inform their online course designs and technology selections. I will then discuss three types of interaction identified in the research—learner–instructor, learner–learner, and learner–content—and use these to structure solutions and planning for online instruction. I will also briefly discuss a fourth type of interaction, learner–environment

(I already addressed much of this in Chapter 2 as a type of self-regulation). I will conclude this chapter by exploring how educators can use research-based principles to support social and emotional learning.

Different Types of Distance

Online learning is a particular form of distance learning, and it is this idea of distance that really needs to be understood if providers are going to design effective instruction and address social and emotional learning in online spaces.

At first, the idea of "distance" seems like a simple one, referring to physical or geographical distance between the teacher and the students. This is an important aspect of distance, but it is only one aspect of distance. In his early work on distance learning, Michael G. Moore (1993) introduced the idea of "transactional" distance, which really elucidated how there are different types of distance. He noted that in addition to the physical or geographic distance, there is a psychological and communication distance. Physical and geographic distance can be bridged by technologies, but psychological and communication distances are bridged through strategies implemented via the technology. Another way of saying this is that technology selection alone does not help you bridge the important emotional and psychological distances with your students. You have to really think about which strategies you want to employ to reduce the sense of distance and then use those strategies to help you select tools that will help you bridge the distances.

Another big difference between the types of distance is that only the physical/geographic distances are truly unique to online learning. The other forms of distance are present in every educational context, including the classroom. Teachers are always trying to bridge a distance with their learners. Even when sitting together in the same room, a person can feel very distant from others.

Physical/Geographic Distance	Psychological/ Communication Distance
Bridged using technology	Bridged using strategies
Unique to online/distance learning	Occurs in every educational context

Over time, transactional distance has expanded to include multiple types of distance: intellectual distance, social distance, and cultural distance, as well as psychological distance and communication distance (Gunawardena & McIsaac, 2004). These distances give rise to misunderstandings and miscommunications (see Figure 3.1). All these distances may seem like a lot to bridge, but they are the distances teachers endeavor to build connections across every day in the classroom. For example, Gunawardena et al. (2019) explore how different cultural values shape learning, and when learners and teachers vary in these values, it creates a type of cultural distance. For instance, how learners and teachers value "errors"

FIGURE 3.1 Different Types of Distance

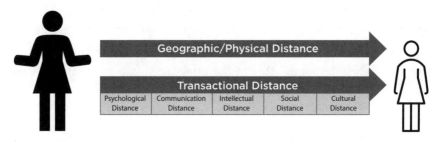

can vary considerably. Some learners or teachers may view errors as serious mistakes that should be minimized, and thus are not valued, while other learners or teachers may value errors or mistakes and see them as opportunities to learn and grow. Another common way in which cultural values shape learning is collaborative learning: in some cultures and classrooms, learning is viewed or valued as an independent activity, and in others learning is viewed and valued as a collaborative process. Learners who view learning as collaborative or have grown up in a culture wherein helping one another with learning is strongly valued can experience a significant degree of cultural distance in a classroom that expects learning to be largely or entirely independent.

Bridging Distance

Bridging different types of distance requires different solutions. For physical and geographic distance, technology helps close the distance gap (see

TABLE 3.1 Bridging Geographic/Physical Distance

GEOGRAPHICAL/PHYSICAL DISTANCE

Bridge Using Technology

Synchronous	*or*	**Asynchronous**	*or*	or a **blend** of
(same time, different place)		(different time, different place)		these

Research does not indicate that any of these options is better or worse— so select what best fits your learners' needs and available infrastructure.

Table 3.1); however, for transactional distance, connections can be created through design and strategies. How you design your course and your lessons, and the strategies that you employ as you do so, make a big difference in your learners' sense of distance. Three general strategies you can use in designing and delivering your online course have a significant impact on learners' sense of distance: structure, dialogue, and autonomy (see Table 3.2).

Structure. How you design and organize your course impacts transactional distance. You always want to have some degree of structure and organization to an online course. The more organized a course is, the greater clarity a student has of what is expected of them and what exactly they need to do when. That said, this can err on the rigid end of the spectrum. In this arena, rigidity refers to the degree of learner input into the course and how responsive the course design is to learners' needs. The more rigid the structure of a course, the greater the sense of distance learners perceive (Moore, 1990;

TABLE 3.2 Bridging Transactional Distances

TRANSACTIONAL DISTANCES
Bridge Using Design and Strategy

Structure	Dialogue	Autonomy
The more inflexible the structure (less responsive to learner needs and inputs), the greater sense of distance learners perceive, but structure is also necessary for learning. In general, young learners require more structure, while older learners more easily adapt to flexible options. ↑ Structure = ↑ Distance ***Goal: Balance structure with dialogue and autonomy***	*The degree of dialogue you foster with your students (with you and between students) impacts their sense of distance. Facilitating dialogue (as a group, individually, in small groups) can lessen the sense of distance.* ↑ Dialogue = ↓ Distance ***Goal: Increase interactions (explored on next pages)***	*Some degree of learner input and control remains desirable. Identify opportunities wherein your students can inform the class design or lead the learning. In general, older students can handle a greater degree of autonomy.* ↑ Autonomy = ↓ Distance ***Goal: Provide increasing or moderate to high degree of learner autonomy, depending on developmental stage and background knowledge***

Dron & Anderson, 2014). As the structure of a course increases, the sense of distance also increases. Since structure is also important for learning, you will want to strive for a balance.

BUILDING YOUR ONLINE LEARNING VOCABULARY

Pacing Versus Modality

One major confusion often arises around the term "asynchronous." People will sometimes confuse "asynchronous" with self-paced, but these terms are not synonymous. One has to do with pacing, the other with modality.

Pacing Options	Modality Options
Self-paced	Synchronous
Class-paced	Asynchronous
Blend of Both	Blend of Both

Synchronous means everyone is participating at the same time but not at the same place. Asynchronous means everyone is participating at different times from different places. Many online classes use both synchronous (live) and asynchronous (on your own schedule) activities and options.

Self-paced means the learner works through the content at their own pace, independent of where any other learners are in the content. Some online learning is designed this way, but a lot of online learning in schools and universities is class-paced. This means the students work through the content at a similar rate. This allows for a much higher degree of interaction between the learners.

Instruction over the course of a week may be a mix of class-paced and self-paced, but the structure from week to week is class-paced. It is possible to have a class that is entirely asynchronous but is class-paced.

First, this means designing a course so that you clearly communicate expectations to students, and you create a rhythm in the course so students can reliably know what to expect both day-to-day and week-to-week. Having clear expectations and a consistent rhythm still leaves a lot of opportunities for student input throughout the course and for designing the course to be responsive to students' needs. Some specific strategies are explored in the section on "social presence." You can also find job aids on *Developing Your Course and Your Communication Plan and Delivering Your Class*, which are in the free handout for this book. Both provide suggestions on ways to create structure and presence in your online classes.

Dialogue. The degree of dialogue you foster with your students also greatly impacts their sense of distance. This includes both their dialogue with you as well as their dialogue with each other. Planning opportunities for dialogue into your course—individually, in small groups, and as a whole class—can reduce the sense of distance. Research shows that as the degree of dialogue goes up, the sense of distance among the learners and instructors goes down (Moore, 1990; Dron & Anderson, 2014; Gunawardena et al., 2019). This may make intuitive sense. Even at a distance, the more you talk with a family member or friend, for example, through email, texts, or video chats, the closer you will feel to that family member or friend. Similarly, the more occasions online learners have to connect with their teachers and other learners and interact with them in meaningful ways, the less they will feel a sense of distance and isolation.

Certainly, there can be too much of a good thing: we don't want to overwhelm learners by requiring too much interaction. But we do want to meaningfully identify what interactions are most helpful for learners and how to integrate those into a course in balanced measure. I will dedicate an entire section of this chapter to types of interaction, and there are job aids in the free handout that can help you think through various options. The main take-away here is that when designing online courses, you will want to increase the degree and nature of interactions to create connectedness in your courses. Otherwise, what you are delivering is simply online content, not online learning.

Autonomy. While degree of learner autonomy may vary with age and prior background knowledge, some degree of learner input and control into the learning process and context is desirable. As with dialogue, the research indicates that as autonomy in an online class increases, the sense of distance decreases.

Complete autonomy is self-paced instruction, and that's not what I'm talking about here. This book is focused on class-paced instruction in which a class is following the same schedule together. But even within class-paced instruction, there are a lot of opportunities for your students to inform the class, help design or plan an activity, and maybe even lead in some way in the class.

This is done quite often in classrooms, too. For example, when you engage your students in developing class rules and expectations together, you are giving your students a degree of autonomy and input into the learning environment. The same reason you want them to have a sense of ownership in the classroom is the same reason you want them to have a sense of ownership in the online class. Identify some ways you can provide autonomy to the learners in your online class: What are some opportunities they have to shape the class, lead a discussion, identify topics of interest, or otherwise have a shared sense of ownership in the class and the learning process? You may have to scaffold autonomy in a class, but you can provide an increased share in creating the learning space over time. Thus, your goal is to provide increasing or a moderate to high degree of learner autonomy, depending greatly on what is appropriate for learner developmental stage and background knowledge.

YOUNGER OR NOVICE LEARNERS AND SELF-REGULATION

In Chapter 2, I talked about the research on self-regulation and the implications of self-regulation for online learning. Self-regulation also has particular relevance for strategies to reduce distance and create connections in our classes.

Young learners or novice learners require more structure. For young learners, you will want to maintain a high degree of dialogue while also providing structure. However, you can still incorporate a great deal of autonomy into the learning environment the same way you would in a classroom. For example, you can ask them to help you create class rules for engagement or let them suggest topics or subtopics to explore.

For novice older and adult learners, it may be good to start with a high degree of structure, but you can slowly reduce the structure and create opportunities for them to lead or organize dialogues and engage in more flexible or adaptive options. For example, you could create a book club toward the end of your class wherein students select a book from a list or suggest a book related to the course and then read together and discuss the book in small groups.

Creating Social Presence

A very important companion concept to transactional distance is "social presence." Social presence means to evoke in your students a sense that you are there for them, you are present, and that a community of learners is also there for them to support each other. Creating social presence in your online classes is key to bridging perceived distances and to fostering and supporting online relationships and learning communities (Short et al., 1976). The degree of social presence in an online class is a strong predictor of student satisfaction with online learning (Gunawardena & Zittle, 1997). Additionally, social presence positively impacts many of the things teachers often worry or wonder about when they are new to online learning: learners' motivation to participate, interactions, group cohesion, trust, verbal and nonverbal communications, and social equality (Kreijns et al., 2011; Richardson & Swan, 2003; Tu, 2001; Whiteside & Garrett Dikkers, 2012). Increasing the amount of dialogue in your course is a general strategy for creating social presence.

Many of the specific strategies you can use to create social presence are the same strategies you can use to support social and emotional learning in online classes. Table 3.3 provides more specific, detailed ideas for how you can create social presence.

TABLE 3.3 Ideas for Creating Social Presence

QUICK IDEAS FOR CREATING SOCIAL PRESENCE	
Introductions	Share an introduction (video, text, or audio, or a mix) and have all learners share an introduction as well. Ask students to share interests or personal trivia they feel comfortable sharing. Make sharing photos optional. Follow up the next week by asking them to read through introductions, and create study groups based on common interests you find.

Class Rules and Expectations	Provide your class with guidelines for "netiquette"; this is a good opportunity to create some "autonomy" by asking them to help generate guidelines and expectations.
Live Audio or Video Chats	Schedule a regular live time and make it a blend of both task-focused and social time; for flexibility, make these optional and record them or meet with students in small groups, based on schedule availability, instead of in one large group.
Student Space	Create a space for students to self-organize and talk with each other; this can be a combination of things like discussion forums where they can post questions and answers, a link to a live room they can meet in 24/7 (like going to the library or a coffee shop together), or using a "presence" tool where they can see who's in the course at the same time as they are and chat with them.
A Class Page	Ask students to cocreate a class page (using Google Docs or something similar) where they share their strengths and interests so they can identify who to reach out to for what.

Types of Interaction Online

Instead of talking about "interaction" as a general concept, it helps to break it down into different types of interaction. This can help you readily identify different ways in which you can facilitate meaningful interactions online. Moore (1989, 1993), in early distance education studies, identified three types of interaction: learner–learner, learner–instructor, and learner–content. There are numerous studies on interaction types, and they are very consistent in suggesting that interaction is an important variable in effective online learning. A few additional interactions have since been identified, such as learner–interface and learner–environment (Gunawardena & McIsaac, 2004). I will discuss four of these types of interaction in depth because there is a solid relationship between these four types of interaction and learning outcomes in and satisfaction with online learning.

Learner-Instructor 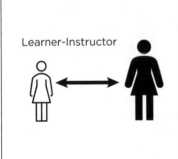	Many of the standards for quality online learning talk about instructor or teacher "presence." This sense of presence comes through how and how often you interact directly with your students. These interactions can be both formal and informal and can occur in a variety of ways. Consistency, timeliness, and responsiveness are key qualities of strong learner–instructor interactions.
Learner-Learner 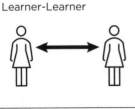	The interactions that take place between learners—both formal and informal—are vital to the learning process. In online learning, identify ways in which students can interact with each other, and structure these so that they are meaningful interactions.

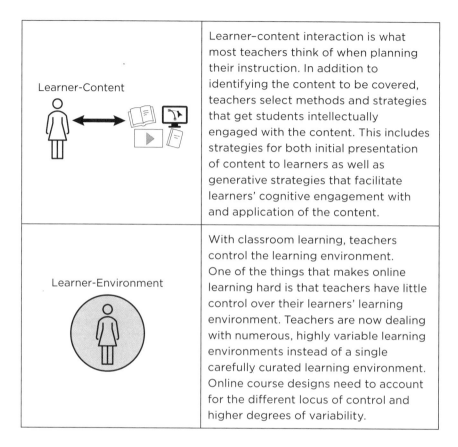

Learner-Content	Learner–content interaction is what most teachers think of when planning their instruction. In addition to identifying the content to be covered, teachers select methods and strategies that get students intellectually engaged with the content. This includes strategies for both initial presentation of content to learners as well as generative strategies that facilitate learners' cognitive engagement with and application of the content.
Learner-Environment	With classroom learning, teachers control the learning environment. One of the things that makes online learning hard is that teachers have little control over their learners' learning environment. Teachers are now dealing with numerous, highly variable learning environments instead of a single carefully curated learning environment. Online course designs need to account for the different locus of control and higher degrees of variability.

Let's look at each of these interaction types in more detail and explore strategies for each.

Learner–Instructor

Most often, the worries of teachers who are new to online instruction center around what the impact will be on that most sacred relationship between teacher and student. The interactions you have with your students that are aimed to bridge the transactional distances discussed earlier are essential to building and preserving these important relationships. You can interact with your students both individually and in groups—both small groups and whole class interactions. The following table (Table 3.4) is a summary of a range of both synchronous and asynchronous options, organized by individual, small-group, and whole-class interactions, to help you think through the various options.

TABLE 3.4 Options for Learner–Instructor Interactions

	INDIVIDUAL	SMALL-GROUP	WHOLE-CLASS
Synchronous	Virtual office hours (use a holding room to make these private individual chats) Periodic brief individual conferences by video, phone, or chat	Live sessions in small groups	Virtual office hours (you can leave the room open for multiple students to come and go) Live sessions (optional) Live sessions (required)

	INDIVIDUAL	SMALL-GROUP	WHOLE-CLASS
Asynchronous	Personal emails—check in with students, gather feedback, provide feedback Formative feedback on student work	Asynchronous forums/discussion boards Formative feedback on group work	Asynchronous forums/discussion boards Weekly summary emails Weekly announcements Recorded talks

How to make good use of synchronous time. With many schools starting the school year online due to COVID-19 or making contingency plans to move to online if there is an outbreak, there is widespread reliance on synchronous instruction. However, the decision to select synchronous online learning requires careful consideration, and implementation of synchronous online teaching requires careful planning—as was explored in Chapter 1. If you are not in a position to decide whether to use synchronous and find that it is required, you can create flexibility within that time to support learners. For example, you can record some direct instruction for the day and ask students to watch that during the first several minutes of synchronous time, and then have students be ready for activities at a different specified point. You can use synchronous time for doing some activities together as a class, and reserve time at the end of the synchronous period for asynchronous activities that students can work on either at that time or at a later time, on their own or in small groups (e.g., in Google Docs), such as focusing on crafting thoughtful responses to a reading or forum prompt or doing other independent activities, while you remain available for questions through live video. This is comparable to letting students have time for independent work or group work or personal choice time in the classroom while you're still accessible to them for questions, clarifications, independent conversations, etc. (you can create a safe place for one-on-one conversations at this time through a breakout room into which you move just yourself and one student).

Teachers also worry about how to support students who are struggling or who are in difficult home situations. Synchronous sessions can present a range of issues—students may not want you or their peers to be able to see into their home lives, or they may not feel comfortable or safe talking with you or they may feel insecure about asking questions to clear up misunderstandings if their learning environments have become troubled spaces. Chris Headleand, a pastor exploring how to provide sensitive pastoral care during remote sessions during the COVID-19 pandemic, provides a good model for how we can think about supporting our struggling learners. He says he begins with the assumption "that people's home environment will be vastly different" (Headleand, 2020, para. 2). He understands full well how home environments introduce situations and circumstances that inhibit sharing. Headleand suggests normalizing the use of different communication options, such as email, chat, video calls, or other options that work well for your students, as some of these may prove easier, more convenient, or more private for your students. By mapping out a range of interactions with your learners—

both synchronous and asynchronous, individually and in small groups, as well as for the whole class—you can normalize a range of communication options that create multiple ways for you to interact with students instead of relying on a way that has, as each method does, its fair share of constraints and drawbacks. In the free online resources provided for this book, I offer some specific ideas on learner–instructor interactions to help you generate ideas and plan for meaningful interactions in your online course.

Once you have identified the types of interaction you want to facilitate between your learners and you, then you can better select the technologies that afford those types of interactions. Often, educators let the term "online learning" limit their thinking about which tools they can use, so it may be more helpful to think of what you're doing as "distance learning" and to leverage a variety of technologies to help you bridge the distance. Some ideas and different tools you can use to facilitate learner–instructor interactions are provided in the sidebar. Often these same tools are also useful for learner–learner and learner–content interaction.

TOOLS FOR LEARNER–INSTRUCTOR
INTERACTION AND INSTRUCTOR PRESENCE

Recorded videos/screencasts—Whether you use software like Camtasia or Screencast-o-matic or you record commentary or narration in a PowerPoint, there are lots of ways you can create presence through recordings.

VoiceThread—Use audio discussions instead of or in addition to text-based discussions—this may be especially helpful for language instruction or working with English-language learners.

Audio feedback—Tools for this method are often available in LMS for you to provide feedback on assignments or responses in discussions.

Video conferencing—This tool allows you and your learners to see each other and interact in real time. Common platforms for this are Zoom, Adobe Connect, WebEx, and Blackboard Collaborate. Use of some of these technologies, however, poses real risks to student privacy and carries potential violation of federal and state laws. If you are going to use Zoom, for example, set up a free K-12 education account, which requires a password by default to enter a meeting and does not permit a user to bypass that requirement. Before you use any of these systems, consult your school or district information technology specialist, and if and when you do use one of them, make sure your students know that taking screenshots or other photos, or making their own recordings, of any class meeting is strictly prohibited.

Asynchronous collaboration—Tools like GoogleDocs, wikis, or other collaboration environments are great ways to provide supportive formative feedback to students as they work on an assignment or a project. Again, however, find out beforehand whether the particular online tool you want to use may violate applicable privacy laws.

Remember: email and phone are also perfectly fine options.

Feedback as a Form of Interaction. Feedback is one of the most important interactions that you can intentionally plan into your online course. I have taught online for nearly 20 years now, and my teaching and my degree of enjoyment in teaching online—as well as my students' satisfaction and learning—greatly improved when I made the conscious move to integrating more opportunities for formative feedback. Feedback is a potent strategy that needs to be used carefully. Feedback that focuses on errors and what students did wrong can have a significant negative impact on motivation, which naturally impacts learning and performance negatively. But feedback that focuses on strategies, including what students did well and where and how they can improve, provides a range of benefits and desirable outcomes.

Strategy-focused formative feedback has a positive impact on student learning and motivation, it decreases their sense of distance in an online course, and it increases their sense of instructor presence as well as their satisfaction with the online learning experience. Instructors who employ formative assessment strategies online also report the feeling that they know their students better and understand their students' needs and how better to help them in the online environment. The more you can incorporate opportunities for this kind of feedback, the stronger your online course will be overall.

Identify opportunities for giving students formative feedback as they work such that they can incorporate your feedback into on-going improvements to their work. You can also have students work in a shareable format like a GoogleDocs where you can check in and provide formative feedback or even just some periodic cheerleading to keep going, but before you do that, read and become familiar with the Google privacy terms that apply to students (https://workspace.google.com/terms/education_privacy.html). Also identify times in the course when students typically have questions about their assignments and create Q&A opportunities in asynchronous discussions, live sessions, or both.

Learner–Learner

As with learner–instructor interactions, learner–learner interactions may be formal or informal. They can occur because you require students to interact through discussions or through collaborations on assignments, and they can occur because students have opportunities to connect on their own. Either way, in online learning, learner–learner interactions are essential and occur when you plan for them and support them. In in-person instruction, these will happen more naturally, but in online learning you must explicitly identify opportunities.

Consider a typical learner–learner interaction in your classroom. While you're trying to explain a new concept in class, one student may lean over to another and say, "I don't get it." The other student may then start to explain it to their friend in a way that's more understandable. We call these specific types of learner–learner interactions "backchanneling." Educators may find backchanneling to be frustrating because it looks and sounds like students are socializing, not listening, but research on backchanneling shows that up to 75% of these conversations are focused on the content and support the learning in some form.

Some research has shown that lack of access to these types of interactions has a negative impact on students' learning and sense of belonging. In a study with girls in STEM, for example, girls who reported a "chilly climate" described environments wherein they didn't feel free to ask fellow students questions, weren't invited to join study groups, and felt like the instructors brushed them off if they had questions after class (Jensen & Deemer, 2019). Just like educators want to create ways for students to ask "after class" questions, we also want to support students in connecting with each other. This connection enhances their learning and understanding and also helps build a learning community.

As educators, we want to create opportunities for both types of learner–learner interactions—formal and informal. There are a range of ways to facilitate student–student interaction. You can use multiple strategies, as appropriate, based on your learner analysis and instructional strategies. The job aid on learner–learner strategies and tools in the free handout for this book can help you generate ideas and map out a plan for learner–learner interactions. Teamwork and group projects are great ways to facilitate learner–learner interaction, and collaboration or team building may be among your class objectives. This can also be great workplace preparation for older students, who may be getting ready to graduate and may be headed to college or looking for jobs. In many industries and businesses today, employees aren't just working in isolation at the office or at home, they are also connecting with colleagues and coworkers remotely to collaborate on projects. In Chapter 4, the section on Teamwork provides further ideas for how to support teamwork and collaboration.

Learner-Content

Learner–content interaction are the methods and strategies used to get learners to engage with content in meaningful ways. It goes beyond reading or watching, which may be just consuming content, to truly interacting with it. When you think about planning instruction, this may be the piece that comes to mind first. Instruction that is designed to get learners engaging with the content—acting on it, not just consuming it—is more effective and more motivating, both in the classroom and online. Estes & Mintz (2016) call this "the law of meaningful engagement" (p. 294). They state that "learners will learn more in proportion to how engaged they are with what they are trying to learn" (p. 294). This involves engaging learners directly with what we want them to learn and providing students frequent opportunities to demonstrate what they have learned (Duckworth, 2006). The goal of instruction is to facilitate understanding and insight as well as to help learners discover how to monitor their learning process and become active participants in guiding it.

There is a range of strategies teachers can use to accomplish meaningful learner–content engagement. I have used ideas from Morrison et al. (2019) to structure ideas around strategies for online learning because their approach makes it easy to see the links from learner characteristics to strategy selection to technology selection.

Two Types of Strategies

You may have taken a methods course that talked about several different methods, such as direct instruction, concept attainment, cooperative learning models, etc. I will organize the discussion on effective learner–content strategies differently. Morrison et al. (2019) created a "Performance–Content Matrix" that can be very helpful in identifying which strategies will be most effective for instruction based on the nature of the content (e.g., are you teaching facts, concepts, principles, procedures, interpersonal skills, or attitudes) and whether your objective is for your learners to recall (remember) or apply what they learn. Within each category, Morrison et al. break down the strategies into two types: initial presentation strategies and generative strategies. You'll find that the methods you have commonly learned fit neatly into one of these two categories.

Initial presentation strategies are strategies you use for introducing the content. They include naming and defining a concept, giving an example or range of examples of a concept, providing an example of a principle or rule in action, demonstrating a procedure, providing a model (e.g., watch a video example), or modeling certain processes or skills.

Generative strategies are strategies you use to help the learner engage with the content to deepen their understanding. These are the strategies you *really* want to get at. Initial presentation is important, but generative strategies engage students' minds with the content. A few examples of generative strategies include using rehearsal-practice (e.g., for spelling), devising mnemonics, asking students to generate examples or definitions (either in addition to what you provide or as a collaborative activity instead of you providing it), asking learners to identify or analyze key characteristics or key ideas, categorizing, generating a concept map, explaining why something works, demonstrating a procedure, and role-playing. All these strategies can be used online as well as in the classroom, and some of them may even be easier to implement in an online environment.

Strategy and Technology Selection

Many times, we use a tool for a presentation strategy that is much more effective as a generative strategy. For example, many instructors defaulted to using Zoom or other synchronous (live) video conferencing tools for initial presentation strategies, but these sorts of tools are much better for generative strategies. For initial presentation of content online, you can record a talk using any number of tools—Camtasia, PowerPoint, iMovie, basic screen recording software on an iPad or other device, and even Zoom, Adobe Connect, Collaborate, etc.—and save it to your class site. Then, during your live video time with students, you can use generative strategies that get students engaging with the content in real time so you can see what issues they run into and answer any questions they have as they're trying to work through things. You can also use asynchronous tools for further generative activities, such as a drag and drop activity or activities wherein students must generate content or examples, record themselves applying a procedure (e.g., a PE activity or a science lab), edit a document that has grammatical and other writing issues, etc.

Let's explore some different ideas for presentation strategies and generative strategies that you can use in online education, based on the type of content you're teaching. I have used the categories in Bloom's taxonomy (Remember, Understand, Apply, Analyze, Evaluate, and Create) to organize these ideas. Sometimes it's easier to envision instruction that facilitates remembering and understanding than instruction that engages application, analysis, evaluation, and creation in an online format, so I've provided several ideas in those categories.

FOR REMEMBER/UNDERSTAND OBJECTIVES

Presentation Strategies: Provide an explanation of the concept or principle, give examples

Presentation Needs and Tools: To present content, you will need the ability either to record explanations that include visuals with audio narration or to present live and share visuals as you talk (e.g., Power-Point or Google slides); wherever possible, try to incorporate examples that include pictures, visuals, and/or videos; try to remove as much text as possible from the screen (labels are fine) to preserve the display area for actual visuals or for carefully sequenced content presentation (you can apply Mayer's multimedia learning principles for your visual content).

Ideas for Generative Strategies and Assessment:

- Knowledge checks (quizzes and tests)—Use periodic quizzes or tests, either during live instruction or by using a quizzing tool, to assess whether students recognize the content, remember what has been covered, and can apply their understanding to a new example or problem.

- Drag and drop activities—Have students do a sorting activity to see how well they understand concepts and differences between multiple concepts; this could be as simple as giving them a Word or Power-Point document wherein they must sort the items under headers or into areas on the page, save their work, and submit it to you; some tools, such as SeeSaw, have activities where students can drag, highlight, write, etc. Again, please consider the privacy implications of specific tools like SeeSaw (https://privacy.commonsense.org/evaluation/seesaw:-the-learning-journal).

- Student-generated content—Ask students to generate a list (e.g., features, criteria, etc.) or multiple lists to demonstrate their understanding of a given concept or different categories. They could do this during a live synchronous session or as an asynchronous activity in a Google Doc or Google Slide.

FOR APPLY/ANALYZE/EVALUATE/CREATE OBJECTIVES

The following is just a sampling of different strategies that have been used in online classes. Hopefully, these will prompt some creative ideas that you can adopt or adapt to your particular class and content.

Presentation Strategies: Using either live video or a recorded video, explain procedures, demonstrate procedures, model thinking aloud as you work on a problem, and/or provide a range of examples across contexts. In some cases, a simulation or a video demonstration may be useful (e.g., application of principles in STEM).

Ideas for Generative Strategies:

- Give students opportunities to practice the procedure and submit their product or effort. They could record themselves doing a procedure or following a process, such as an at-home lab or a new exercise, or take pictures of projects at different stages or of final products.
- Ask students to explain the steps of a procedure or to explain their process while they demonstrate their performance in a video—that is, a talk-aloud of solving a math problem, of working on an experiment, or of thinking their way through a design challenge.

- Ask students to analyze a recorded demonstration in which they apply principles from readings, record an analysis of something such as a written document or piece of art, or submit a written analysis.
- Simulations provide a lot of opportunities for students to test and/or manipulate different ideas. For STEM, there are a lot of existing simulations and labs on www.merlot.org, https://phet.colorado.edu, and www.labxchange.org.
- Ask students to generate examples and/or instances in which the methods or procedures being studied are applicable (and, perhaps, when they are not applicable, to facilitate decision making). Students could submit answers via an online quiz with an open-ended question, perhaps using Google Docs, or students could generate ideas together as a group, either synchronously or in a shared document they submit to you.
- Have students do some "citizen science," wherein they gather data from "the field" by gathering items or data near their home or on a nature walk. During safer times, when students can go do things in the community, you could ask them to visit sites and record "reports from the field" or conduct interviews with community leaders.
- Many museums and nonprofits have virtual exhibits and virtual learning opportunities created during 2020. You could select virtual museum exhibits or virtual field trips that align with your content and ask students to complete those activities, report on their learning, then create their own activity or work of art on the topic that they can share virtually.

Ideas for Assessment:

- Ask students to explain back to you, either during a live or recorded video, their understanding of the procedure.

- Have students create a concept map or visual model and either submit it or meet with you individually to give a 5 minute presentation, wherein you have an opportunity to gauge their understanding and provide feedback.

- Ask students to write and submit a synopsis explaining what principles were applied where and how.

- Create a discussion board where students can share recordings of them giving a tour or explanation of their work.

- For exercises/stretches or labs (e.g., for PE or science, respectively), ask students to record themselves doing an exercise or completing an experiment or lab-related activity, such as building a prototype or testing and gathering data, and submit the video or connect on live video to demonstrate their accomplishment and get immediate feedback. Make sure you are keeping these recordings behind a secure firewall on a learning management system where they are available only within your class. You also should make sure you know your school's policies about sharing video recordings of students in class, including whether your students' caregivers' consent is required and has been given. Even if your students' caregivers have given consent in the forms that they filled out at the start of the school year, you may want to let them know about your plans for the recording and sharing of videos in your online class and verify their consent.

- Ask students to produce an authentic product (design, work of art, lab report, business plan) and then share it in small breakout rooms during a live class session for feedback and on-going development or iterations of their work. You could also ask students to create their own exhibits of their work, using tools such as artsteps.com or www.3dvas.com, or have them assemble a digital portfolio of their work.

FOR AFFECTIVE OBJECTIVES

Use of examples, role-playing, case studies, simulations, and diverse teams are all possible strategies (that can be used independently or in conjunction) for affective learning objectives. The following examples may help you draft ideas for your class:

- Talk through multiple examples (worked examples, demonstrations, talk-aloud on how you solved a problem, etc.) that provide students insight into a range of different ways people have solved a similar problem or used different strategies.
- Create a role-playing situation where students take on different roles or stakeholder groups in a scenario, then structure the live class time for deliberation, discussion, or negotiation (while you facilitate, summarize, etc.).
- Provide students with multiple case studies or scenarios that reflect different features, situations, or approaches, and ask them to decide what to do in each case or to analyze the cases then generate their own examples.
- Some simulations can be useful for affective objectives, especially if teamwork is involved or if working with people from other cultures is among the objectives. Give students an authentic problem they must

work on together to solve. They could work as a group, or you could even form small groups that represent diverse stakeholders related to the problem and require those groups to negotiate with each other towards a solution. Their interactions could include both asynchronous research and preparation as well as synchronous deliberation and negotiation.

- Consider which sort of diversity is central to your objective— disciplinary, cultural, skill/capability, racial, geographic, etc.—and select examples or design activities to highlight differences and that require learners to consider these differences as they problem solve.

Examples of Generative Strategies in Practice

Worked Examples/Demonstration: A science teacher records a talk introducing a new concept and the equation associated with that new concept. He records himself writing on his iPad and talking as he works through the problem. He saves this recording and uploads the video, along with another problem related to this same concept, for students work on then submit. Then during a live session, he introduces yet another problem related to the new concept—this one more complex—and asks the students to work on it in small breakout groups during their live session. He checks in on the groups as they work, then he has them return to the main room and share their work; then he wraps up by addressing issues and questions he saw arise during the class session.

This content area example can readily be adapted to SEL objectives. Instead of a math-based problem, you could present an example of a social or emotional challenge you have had or have helped a student with and talk through how you or you and that student worked on the problem: what strategies you or they employed, how it went, what was learned. After recording yourself, you can upload the video and give your students the asynchronous assignment of writing out ideas about how they would handle that same or another given situation. Depending on the nature of the problem you present, you could then have students share their ideas in small groups during a live video session, then share what happened in the small groups with the whole class to identify a range of strategies. If the topic is one that you feel the content may be too sensitive for students to personalize, you could provide students a *case study/scenario* with your video and have students write up an analysis of that case study/scenario asynchronously, then discuss it during a live session using a small-group or whole-group structure.

Role-Playing: For a government class, students are learning about community engagement processes. The teacher decides she wants the students to take on different perspectives of stakeholders in the local community and go through the same process of deliberation and decision making used by their local city council. To do this, she identifies the different stakeholder groups in the community and creates teams for each stakeholder group, assigning each student to one of these groups. The students then research their assigned stakeholder perspective and write a statement paper asynchronously in their small groups using Google Docs. She reviews the statements and provides initial feedback. Then during their live class session, the class uses their time to deliberate between groups. She gives them the goal of reaching an agreement or decision by the end of class, then allows each group a few minutes to present their positions and the rest of the class period to deliberate and decide.

Role-playing is a great strategy for helping students develop social and emotional skills. Most of the planning for this is thinking through what students should be able to produce by the end of the class period, what the different perspectives will be, assigning students to these different roles or groups, and then providing them with a structured assignment so they can engage effectively. You can have them engage asynchronously, through discussions and generation of a shared product, or you can have them engage synchronously, in a discussion wherein they work to solve the problem together. You could also engage students in identifying a problem they want to tackle, work with them to identify the different stakeholder groups and perspectives, then put them into groups to work together from there.

Learner-Environment

For many teachers new to online education, this is the first time they have had to think about their students' learning *environments* in a new way. With classroom learning, teachers control the learning environment. One of the things that makes online teaching hard is that teachers no longer have direct control over the learners' learning environment. Teachers are also now dealing with numerous, highly variable learning environments instead of a single carefully curated one. Online course designs need to account for a different locus of control and high degrees of variability.

I discussed on this a great deal in Chapter 2 in connection with self-regulation. To recap Chapter 2, there are some strategies teachers can use to help learners build an environment that will facilitate their learning. Educators can help learners manage their distracting learning environments through direct instruction and generative, active learning in which students generate ideas for managing their home learning environments, identify possible issues, and brainstorm solutions (on their own, with each other, and/or with a caretaker). I presented the example in which LaToya Sapp asked students to share their favorite learning spots at home and talk about what makes for a great learning spot. Sapp also shared her favorite learning spot at home to model this sort of self-regulation. By creating direct instruction and class activities in which students explicitly think through how they can manage distractions and other needs in their learning environment, you can help them develop effective strategies. You may wish to revisit the section in Chapter 2 on self-regulating the learning environment to identify additional strategies for supporting your students in their learner–environment interactions.

Connections to SEL Teaching Practices

The discussions in this chapter related/applied to five of Yoder's teaching practices for SEL: student-centered discipline, responsibility and choice, warmth and support, classroom discussions, and balanced instruction.

Student-Centered Discipline

Many of the strategies for and examples of facilitating interactions presented in this chapter place an emphasis on supporting student-centered discipline. By providing establishing routines, involving students in setting course rules and expectations, and providing multiple communication channels for different types of interaction, you can create a student-centered approach to discipline and classroom management.

FIGURE 3.2 Example of a student choice board for a high school history course with some SEL and self-care activities. Created and shared by Alicia Hatmaker, Social Studies Teacher at Athens Drive Magnet High School (Raleigh, NC). March 2020. Used with permission.

CRASHCOURSE US HISTORY	THE CORONAVIRUS AUDIO DIARY PROJECT—WEEK 1	PERSONAL READING
Review Unit 1 of American History so far with a CrashCourse video—pause to take notes as you need to! *Video Links:* Colonizing America, Natives and the British, and The American Colonies	Record an audio note answering this week's "Coronavirus Audio Diary" questions. Be sure to read all of the instructions before you submit! QUESTIONS HERE SUBMIT HERE	Read at least 19 pages from a book of your choosing. Take a picture with your book (be creative!) and email it to Ms. Hatmaker with a brief summary of what you read for a social media shoutout!
WATCH A TED TALK Watch a TEDTalk of your choosing and take notes! Use questions from your TEDTalk Form to help you further analyze and critique the video.	**AMERICAN HISTORY I** ***STUDENT CHOICE BOARD*** **Directions:** 1. Complete as many of the squares as you can, in any order you choose. 2. Use the "fill" tool to color in each box as you complete it. Just highlight the square and click on the paint bucket to fill. If you don't see the paint bucket, click on the three dots on the top right of the screen. 3. Take breaks!! Don't try to finish everything quickly. Pace yourself! 4. Have fun! *Ms. Hatmaker's* *"Office Hours"* *are M–F from 1–3pm!*	**WATCH CNN10 EACH DAY** To stay informed about current events around the world, spend 10 minutes each day watching CNN10 with a family member. Once a week, check in with Ms. Hatmaker during office hours to chat about it!
TRY A GUIDED MEDITATION Guided Meditation for HS Students Spend 10 minutes using the guided meditation above if you need to take a mental break and unwind!		**LEARN A NEW LANGUAGE!** Download the DuoLingo or Babbel app and start practicing for 15min a day! **All students can get three months of Babbel for free—get details here!
FIND A NEW SONG TO LOVE Listen to a playlist that's a bit outside of your normal comfort zone. If you hear something cool, email it to Ms. Hatmaker for a future "song of the day"!		**PLAY A KAHOOT** Review your knowledge of the early American colonies using the Challenge mode on Kahoot! Play here or join using code.
TAKE A VIRTUAL FIELD TRIP Explore the world while still being self-quarantined with a virtual field trip to the Jamestown Settlement!	**REVIEW USING KHAN ACADEMY** Review THREE online modules for Thinking Like a Historian, New and Old Worlds Collide, and the Early American Colonies (1607–1754). There are readings, videos, and practice questions. Take the unit assessment at the end to see which areas you're doing great in and which may need further review!	**MOVE AROUND!** Get your body moving with a 30min HIIT Cardio Workout, a beginner's yoga session, a Latin dance workout, or going for a walk/run!

Responsibility and Choice

Similar to the idea of autonomy discussed in this chapter, responsibility and choice relates to identifying how you can put democratic norms in place in your class. How can your students choose different options and have some input into the class? For example, structure a lesson so that within that structure, students can pick the topics they want to focus on or learn more about. Choice boards, like the example in Figure 3.2, are an excellent approach for providing structured choice and also building in flexible options for some SEL activities. Use small groups for students to share their learning or develop arguments with supporting evidence and to get feedback from peers. In an online class, you can use breakout rooms for these activities. Be sure to scaffold the peer process with a document that provides some structure as they exercise choice.

Warmth and Support

Presence is all about warmth and support. As you create presence through teacher–student interactions, ask questions of students that show you are listening. Follow up with them, through a one-on-one email or phone call, when they have a problem or concern. Community strategies, covered in Chapter 4, can also help communicate warmth and support.

Classroom Discussions

As you may have already gathered, classroom discussions are a cornerstone practice for online instruction. These are where the discussions around content happen, where you can observe students immediately in synchronous discussions or see how well they can integrate and elaborate in an asynchronous discussion. Using both live (synchronous) and asynchronous discussions will help students practice different types of communication skills—verbal and written—as well as afford you opportunities to model communications skills. These are great practice opportunities not just for academic content but also for SEL content.

Balanced Instruction

Yoder explains that balanced instruction means using an appropriate mix of direct and active instruction. In Chapter 1, I explained how the SAFE practices reinforce a balanced instructional approach. In the student–content interaction section in this chapter, the two different strategies I introduced—presentation and generative—are direct instruction and active instruction. This practice of combining presentation (direct) and genera-tive (active) strategies will help you design balanced instruction. If you are already applying those in your instructional planning, good news—you are employing balanced instruction online.

Summary

A sense of physical or geographic distance may be the most obvious form of distance, but it's also the easiest to address by selecting technologies that help you connect with your learners. You may want to select some technologies that aren't online tools, depending on your learners' needs. More importantly, as teachers we want to address psychological, emotional, intellectual, and cultural forms of distance—"transactional distances"—that arise in all teaching and learning environments. By understanding these types of distance, teachers can choose effective strategies for bridging the various types of distance.

One main idea for bridging distance is creating social presence. Teachers create social presence through interactions with their learners—it is through these interactions that students sense that the teacher is there and paying attention to them, their needs, and their work and that others are sharing the same learning experience. Specifically, there are four types of interaction educators want to attend to or help learners attend to in online learning: learner–instructor, learner–learner, learner–content, and learner–environment. Some planning tools have been provided to help you create an interaction plan for your class. By mapping out your plan for each of these types of interaction, you are building a robust foundation for a meaningful online learning experience that can support SEL and your learners' success in the online environment.

That there are types of interactions is one of the most interesting insights to come out of research on effective online teaching and learning. In addition to providing three easy-to-remember ideas you can use to design engaging online instruction, these same types of interaction also take place in your classroom and in blended learning environments. You can start to use the types of interaction for mapping out when, where, and how you want students to interact with the content, with you, and with each other, and then identify which tools would be best for facilitating (i.e., affording) the desired interactions.

Creating Community Online

Throughout the preceding chapters, I have continually discussed the idea of community in online learning. Let's take a deeper look at different ideas for how you can create a learning community online.

Two Views of Online Education: Individualized Versus Social Learning Approaches

There are two very different philosophies and approaches to online learning. You have no doubt heard the terms I'm about to discuss used interchangeably by vendors, but I want to provide you with a research-based structure for thinking about these philosophies. Not only will this help you think about how you design your classes, but it will also help you analyze different tools and sales pitches to better understand what type of learning experience they're promoting. This can help you quickly evaluate the dizzying array of technologies and select those that support you in accomplishing the vision you have for your class, school, or district.

Individualized Instruction
(Including Personalized or Self-Directed Learning)

One vision that is commonly advanced for online learning is individualized instruction. Individualized instruction is an approach to learning wherein an instructor or expert establishes the learning objectives and the content, but the learner determines the pace and may even be able to choose the sequence. The learner takes an individualized path through the content. You can think of this as self-paced instruction, in which the learner moves through instruction at their own pace, but the content has been carefully designed and planned for them. Online education comes up a lot around this sort of approach to learning because online systems can be used to deliver content in a highly individualized way. Students read through and listen to content, take a quiz or test, and based on the results, move on, revisit content, etc. This is also called "adaptive learning" because it adapts to the learners' needs and knowledge level. A further extension of this idea is personalized instruction, wherein the learner determines everything—the objectives, the content, pacing, etc. It is sometimes called self-directed learning because the learner is in control of every aspect of their learning.

It is helpful to think about these terms in relation to what types of outcomes they best support. Individualized instruction is focused on content mastery. Learners are assessed at the levels of Remembering and Understanding, using Bloom's taxonomy to help frame this examination. There may be some instances when it makes most sense—based on a learner's needs or goals or other circumstances—to give learners the option to master content in an individualized fashion. More often, we see this used with adult learners, such as in trainings to develop new skills.

Personalized learning, on the other hand, is perhaps best thought of as a form of lifelong learning, whether it takes place independently or as part of formal schooling. We engage in self-directed learning when we decide to learn a new language, to learn how to cook a new type of cuisine, to take up a new form of yoga, and so on. The internet can be very supportive of self-directed, personalized learning, whether the opportunities are informal or within the more formal school curriculum. For example, for an independent learning class in high school, my son chose to work on a hydroponics project, and he watched YouTube videos of farmers talking about various approaches, setups, technical details, crops, etc. He generated his own objectives, directed his own learning, and sorted through available information on his own, even within the more formal context of school. For another example, I decided to learn how to cook Middle Eastern cuisine and have been learning through books, videos, and blogs by those sharing their practices online, all outside of any formal learning context. Personalized learning may happen in the context of day-to-day life as we seek to learn new things and to grow, or it may happen embedded within a formal learning environment in the form of self-directed projects that students get to work on.

Because they are self-paced and sometimes even self-directed, these forms of online learning can be isolating. When teachers try to transform classes into one of these models, the end result can be especially isolating. It's one thing for an individual to decide they want to learn something new and choose to watch videos or read blogs on it. It's another thing entirely for them to choose to be part of a learning community but end up in a situation where they have no opportunities to connect with others. Individualized and personalized learning have a time and a place, but neither of these is usually implied in discussions about online learning.

Social Online Learning—Class-based, class-paced

A whole separate philosophy and body of work starts with the theory that learning is social and that a learning community is important to the process. In formal education, a social theory of learning is a much more common philosophy that informs the design of online learning. From this perspective on online learning, students are in a class with other learners, working and learning at the same pace and often working together in some manner. Even in an asynchronous class, students are working through the class at the same weekly pace even if they are working according to their own schedules within a given week, and they are interacting with each other and collaborating on projects, but doing so at times convenient to their schedules. Social online learning features a high degree of interaction with the content, with fellow students, and with the instructor. These classes can be asynchronous, synchronous, or both. (In truth, synchronous classes always have some asynchronous components like readings or individual work or group work outside of class time. It's extremely rare to see a class that is purely synchronous. Even classroom-based learning assumes time outside of class.)

These distinctions are particularly important for SEL online. If you want to tend to SEL needs and objectives in an online class, then you will want to actively select a social approach to online learning. Many of the strategies that were discussed in Chapter 3 are rooted in a social learning philosophy and approach to online learning. In fact, the types of interactions and idea of social presence discussed in Chapter 3 stem from the a framework that is based on the social philosophy of online learning: Community of Inquiry. Let's dig deeper into this framework, as it can be helpful for going beyond the interactions to truly building a learning community online through which you help your students feel connected and supported.

Community of Inquiry—A Social Framework for Online Learning

In 2000, Garrison et al. first introduced the Community of Inquiry (CoI) model for online learning (we have been studying and designing online learning environments for over 20 years). Early educational philosophers C.S. Pierce and John Dewey had advanced the idea of a community in the educational setting (Beckett, 2019; Pardales & Girod, 2013), and Garrison et al. (2000) adapted this idea to online learning. CoI is grounded in the idea that the social context significantly affects the nature of the learning process and its outcomes (Resnick, 1991). A learning community is particularly important for higher-order learning and is requisite for processes and objectives like deliberation, negotiating meaning, analyzing misconceptions, and challenging assumptions and beliefs (Lipman, 1991). A sense of community also supports persistence and satisfaction with online learning (Richardson et al., 2017). Garrison et al. (2000) proposed the following model (Figure 4.1) for Community of Inquiry, and this model has been very stable over the past 20 years.

I talked about social presence in Chapter 3. Social presence is simply the ability to perceive others in an online environment as real and to project oneself as a real person too—which is in contrast to feeling like you're interacting with avatars, unknown people, or a computer. Social presence involves open communication as well as affective expressions and group cohesion. One comment I hear from time to time is that a lot of communication cues are lost online, and often folks refer to nonverbal expressions. However, you can readily address this by incorporating affective expressions into your communications in an online class. For example, I often incorporate emojis or text emojis such as :-) as well as nonverbal expressions like {smile} or {grin} or {she says sarcastically}, and I translate physical reactions into written expressions like "Cheering for you!"

Supporting discourse, which is the space where social presence and cognitive presence overlap, can help address some of these communication concerns. Much of what I covered in Chapter 3 will support discourse, but some general strategies for facilitating discourse include connecting ideas, identifying misconceptions and helping students untangle misunderstandings, and asking students to clarify statements or ideas. In addition,

FIGURE 4.1 Community of Inquiry Framework. Reprinted from *The Internet and Higher Education*, Vol. 2, D. Randy Garrison, Terry Anderson, Walter Archer, 87–105, Copyright 1999, with permission from Elsevier.

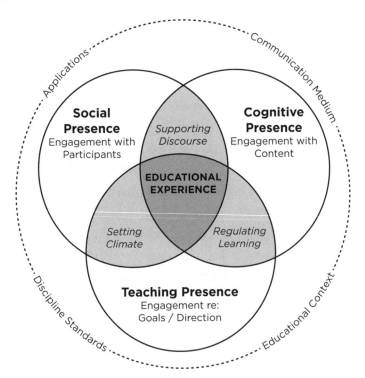

modeling social presence cues for your learners supports the learning environment by creating a culture of collaboration and trust, which encourages participation. As suggested earlier, encouragement is an important form of social presence that also supports student engagement with the content (Rovai, 2007). Other social presence cues include addressing students by name, modeling the sharing of your opinion and experiences in the manner you want students to, and sharing personal stories or reflections that serve the purpose of enhancing the learning community (Bassani, 2011; Molseed, 2011).

Teaching presence refers to how you design, facilitate, and direct the learning process in your class. It's about how you design the course, how it's organized, what activities you incorporate or create, how you assess the learning, how you facilitate activities and interactions, and any direct instruction you provide. You create not just the presence of a person (social) but the presence of a teacher who is structuring and supporting the learning process. Learners pick up on this presence through each of your instructional decisions and actions. I have talked about how to carefully plan your instruction both generally for online education and specifically for SEL. These practices establish your teaching presence.

Cognitive presence has to do with learner–content interactions, which was covered in Chapter 3. Cognitive presence is the extent to which learners can construct meaning and confirm, disconfirm, and adjust through reflection and interaction. The goal of Social Presence and Teaching Presence is to stimulate Cognitive Presence—really getting learners to meaningfully engage with the content through active learning.

I have already extensively covered supporting discourse and regulating learning in Chapters 1 and 2, so I will discuss setting climate next.

Setting Climate

Parker and Herrington (2015) developed user-friendly design principles for "setting climate" in online learning based on findings from research:

1. Create a user-friendly learning environment (physical environment)
   - Develop an easy-to-follow navigation menu
   - Employ an uncluttered design style
   - Organize flow of information and materials in a logical manner
2. Build a positive rapport (social presence)
   - Decrease psychological distance (isolation): Use open friendly communication (verbal and nonverbal)
   - Encourage connectedness: Be an active participant, and offer opportunities for interaction (student–facilitator and student–student)
   - Express your personality: Self-disclose some personal information (e.g., hobbies, favorite travel destinations)
   - Be approachable: Articulate your availability, advise how students can contact you, and respond promptly
   - Develop mutual trust: Show respect, courtesy, and patience
3. Engender a sense of belonging (emotional expression)
   - Address students by name
   - Encourage students to participate
   - Recognize and praise progress and achievement

4. Promote a sense of purpose (instructional management)
    ▪ Articulate goals
    ▪ Monitor performance
    ▪ Give helpful advice
    ▪ Provide constructive feedback

I have already discussed many of these practices in the sections on how to bridge distance and create social presence. One practice I haven't discussed much is the user-friendly environment. Creating a user-friendly online education environment relates to how you set up your course site in your LMS. In general, you want to make sure that you make it easy for your learners to access content and resources and that you organize your home page, weekly/unit modules, and content in such a way that it is easy for learners to find what they're looking for. For my courses, I like to create a home page that includes a welcome message and links to important documents (e.g., the syllabus and assignment handouts students will need to access throughout the course). You could incorporate a welcome video on the home page or in the first week's module, wherever you think it most appropriate. I also like to keep the course menu as short and uncluttered as possible and to embed links to files, videos, and details within weekly modules. Where possible, I also prefer to use a single landing page for each week rather than a bunch of separate tools and items that leave students clicking all around to find one bit of information. Table 4.1 is a template that mirrors how I lay out my home pages for my online courses (note that some LMSs

TABLE 4.1 Sample template for course home page layout

Course Menu: Syllabus Modules Discussion Gradebook Announcements		*(Create an organizing visual or a graphic for the class as part of your home page; this helps learners immediately recognize when they are on your class site.)*
	Overview & Welcome *(Incorporate a quick class overview with some instructions for students, such as what to look for on the menu or where to go first). Also include a warm welcome message. You may also want to record a welcome video that includes a tour of the course site and link to it from here.)* Welcome video!	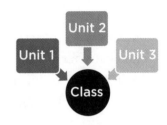

	Quick Links to Documents & Assignment Handouts/Rubrics
	
	(I always include quick links to the main documents and assignment details students should have. This way, they can get right to it on the main page without always have to dig for it or remember exactly which week it is.)
	• Course syllabus
	• Main Course Project Handout
	  ▪ Assignment 1 Details & Rubric
	  ▪ Assignment 2 Details & Rubric
	  ▪ Assignment 3 Details & Rubric
	• Journal Handout & Rubric
	• Portfolio Details & Rubric
	• Participation Rubric	

TABLE 4.2 Example weekly page layout, linking to everything from one spot

Course Menu:	Week 1 Overview	*My Post-It Note Area*
Syllabus **Modules** **Discussion** **Gradebook** **Announcements**	*(Overview content goes here, and write out for students what they should do this week. If you have any recorded talks, link to them here or under the "Readings & Videos" box below. Think of this space as the outline you want to provide.)* *(For the blue boxes below (or whatever color you pick), I create a Course Schedule in the course syllabus and then use that same Schedule structure. So, in some courses, I may have four blue boxes instead of three. This helps to organize and chunk information and directs students through the content in the sequence I want them to follow.)*	*(Sometimes during a given week, I may want to have a "post-it" sort of reminder or note for students. In those instances, I'll add a yellow box to the side like this with the relevant information or links. For example, if I want them to be thinking about their paper topic this week so they can submit a proposal next week, I would put that here.)*

Readings (& Videos)	**Weekly Discussions & Live Meetings**	**Weekly Assignments**
• Required readings • Handouts • Videos	• Link to discussion • Link to group project • Link to live meeting • Office hours: (link)	• Due Date: Submit Here (links to the Assignment in LMS) **Assignment Resources:** • Handout & Rubric • Example(s)

provide a cleaner interface than others, so some of this may be hard to do in a few of the more popular LMSs).

I prefer to keep the home page for my courses very simple—just enough stuff for them to know they're on the right page and quickly get to information they need throughout the course. Adding white space helps to chunk the information and make it more readable, and headers that are in a larger and different color font help learners quickly organize and integrate the information.

For each weekly module, I create a single page that links out to everything the students will need and that has designated spaces (see Figure 4.2 for an example). You could organize these by weeks or by units with separate weeks under the units, but students find it easier when all information for a given week or unit is on the same page. They spend less time hunting and frustrated and more time focused on the content.

Ideally, students would never be more than one or two clicks away from anything. This is harder to do in some LMSs, but if you can create pages and link to elements in your course site in your LMS, consider an approach like this.

Going From Presence to Community

While creating presence and facilitating interactions lay an excellent foundation for creating community, there are additional strategies you can use to build a supportive learning community. For online learning, having a learning community helps learners to further develop their self-regulation (Lin et al., 2016) and increases their motivation to cope with tasks and the learning process through peer support and feedback (Chang et al., 2013). Time spent in communication activities is also a strong predictor of persistence and completion of online learning (Rienties & Toetenel, 2016).

COMMUNITY ONLINE: SHARED CREATION OF A SHARED SPACE

(From Moore, 2020—Designing Interactive Online Learning, A Quick Reference Guide.)

Create Sharing Time

Even with younger learners, while using Zoom or live sessions, you can leave the first few minutes to be social time. As the students join, sit back for just a bit and let them chat and connect like they would in the classroom. After they have had some social time, you can bring everyone together as a class for more structured time. You could, additionally or alternatively, designate times when you will all meet that will be entirely social with an open structure.

Create Sharing Space

Create a course page, a class wiki (Google Doc), or other space where students can own and share and create course content. Give them dedicated discussions or forums, maybe a link to a video chat room they can use any time, where they can generate together, initiate discussions on their own, and support each other. Many LMSs have tools you can use to create a group space that includes common collaboration tools just for that group.

Share the Creating

Explicitly invite students to contribute and give presentations or share something they have found or learned with the rest of the class. Get your students involved in helping you design this space as well—ask them for feedback on what they want and ask for volunteers to help organize or facilitate.

Building online community is sort of like building a local geographic community; in order to thrive, your community needs infrastructure that is both clear and transparent enough that community members see it and will use it—and flexible enough that they feel they can shape it and "inhabit" it. Think of various community spaces in your local community. There are different types of places and spaces for engaging in different types of activities. A library is a wonderful metaphor to think of for virtual communities. Libraries do not define what their patrons do with the space, but they do provide different types of spaces in a resource-rich environment that supports reading, getting information (computers), quiet spaces for reading, and spaces for group work or families reading together.

Often, a teacher will have a space, or spaces, set aside in their classroom for different types of activities, and you could adopt the same metaphor into your online class. Like the example in Chapter 1, a simple visual where you label a tool or space for students to use can go a long way toward creating community spaces in your class. In fact, if you know that your learners will be returning to your classroom at some point or if you are designing blended instruction, mapping some features of your classroom into your online class can help students easily transition from one environment to the other. Let's look at specific strategies you can use for facilitating community in your online class.

Strategies for Facilitating Community Online

Week 1—Setting the Tone

If building a learning community is a priority for you in your class, then you want to start doing so in Week 1 of your class. The following are some Week 1 activities you can use to help build community. These are best used in tandem, but you can select a few, in the interest of time, if necessary:

- ❐ Orientation activity—getting to know the class environment
- ❐ Orientation activity—getting to know each other (shared interests and goals)
- ❐ Create a class community space—single place where students can share information and find others with shared interests, etc.
- ❐ Create a discussion for class introductions—include a prompt to share interests

❑   Class activity—define the desired class community; generate course
     guidelines and protocols/etiquette

❑   Once you have laid the groundwork for a learning community, the
     following are various ideas and strategies you can use throughout the
     rest of your class to foster and support an online community (adapted
     from Gunawardena et al., 2019).

Teacher and Student Introductions: Introductions build connectedness.
Have students share introductions in a discussion forum and ask questions
or share similar interests. One technique you could use is storytelling: Ask
students to write or record a story. Give them the option of including a pho-
tograph or a representative image. For example, for younger learners, ask
students to share a picture of their favorite toy or stuffed animal who will be
their "learning buddy." Again, make sure that these photos or videos reside
behind a firewall in a secure learning management system.

Cybercafé: For older students, a virtual space where they can meet for informal and social chats can develop a sense of camaraderie. Akin to meeting
in a coffee shop, the cybercafé is an unmoderated discussion where participants can discuss topics of interest to them.

Community Space: As suggested in Chapter 3, give your students a dedicated
space. For example, students could cocreate a webpage or Google Doc to summarize their talents and strengths. They can share stories, short videos, and
engage in other cultural exchanges to enrich learning about the community.

If you're concerned about students making unhelpful edits to others' work, set community rules of engagement first before students work on these projects. Additionally, a benefit to a tool such as Google Docs is that it retains a history of the edits on a document and who made them. This allows you to see what edits were made, by whom, when, and restore edits that should not have been removed. If necessary, you may even want to revisit activities and discussions on regulating interactions with others, as discussed in Chapter 2 or meet individually with students who exhibit challenges while collaborating with others.

Desktop or Mobile Conferencing: Provide students some flexible time during synchronous (real-time/live) sessions. Some teachers dedicate the first 5 minutes or last 10 minutes of a live class session to social time for students to chat and share.

Netiquette: As mentioned elsewhere, establishing etiquette guidelines for the class is important to community building. By engaging students in the discussion, you support them in making it their own.

Create Peer Support Groups: In the first week, establish small (e.g., 3–4 students) peer support groups that will be their go-to group for any questions or support outside of class. You can let them create their own groups or you can create the groups for them. In your LMS, you may have a specific Group tool that allows you to create space for each group—this will give them a space that includes tools they can use for collaboration and discussion, such as file sharing and a discussion board only their group members can see (you will be able to see all groups' discussions and files). Provide them with guidelines or have them generate their group guidelines together and submit those to you by the end of the first week. Using introductions to identify diverse strengths, create groups that mix strengths; have the groups share their strengths and explore how to maximize their strengths as a group. Provide the groups with a video on how to use technology to support their teamwork as well as tips for collaboration.

Give Permission to Socialize: Students often feel unsure about what tools are okay to use and how to use them in an online class. Explicitly tell students they can use their community or group spaces both for class work and as spaces to decompress, destress, and socialize.

Create an Open Questions Space: In addition to a community sharing space, make sure you have a place where everyone can post either general questions on anything they are confused about or interesting course-related information they've heard or read about and want to share. Make sure you set aside time to check this space regularly to address any questions.

Teamwork—Information Sharing to Cooperation to Collaboration

Often, we want our students to truly collaborate, but achieving collaboration requires some scaffolding. Research on collaboration identifies three levels of teamwork: information sharing (exchanging information), cooper-

ation (work is divided and everyone completes their parts), and collaboration (team members plan together and produce a final product or outcome
together; Dillenbourg, 1999; Blau, 2011). Learners may cooperate but not
truly collaborate due to a sense of ownership (e.g., they lack a sense of ownership for the project or feel responsible only for their part) or conditions
that externally motivate performance (e.g., grading structure and policies)
that sends a message that students will be graded individually for their
work. More conscientious students will want to make sure they can complete their work successfully without their work being impacted by less
conscientious students. Structure the process and your grading and policies
to support collaboration or to reflect *both* cooperation and collaboration. For
example, CATME is a suite of online tools and supports designed to support
teamwork, and they have tools that allow group members to rate each other.
You could structure the work so that students receive both an individual
grade for their portion of the work and a collaboration grade based on their
peer ratings and feedback.

As Blau et al. (2020) note, "when rooted in appropriate pedagogy, digital tools play an important role in communication in learning communities.
These tools promote ubiquitous and persistent connectivity and support the
practice of regular exchange of ideas and insights, as well as digital collaboration, by offering asynchronous and synchronous shared workplaces" (p. 7).
To help students with teamwork, you will want to structure any teamwork
such that the groups have opportunities to ask questions, provide input,
resolve disagreements, negotiate, and build understanding together (Blau

& Shamir-Inbal, 2017). You can explicitly structure weekly group activities to begin with writing out questions the first week, then for the next week or two students provide input to questions and ideas, then during the next few weeks you meet with groups in breakout rooms or in small groups via live video conferencing to check in and see what disagreements or disputes have arisen and help them resolve these disputes; which provides you the opportunity to integrate and model SEL objectives. After that, facilitate any necessary negotiation within the group then give them time to wrap up and submit a cocreated final product or outcome. If you want to build some group work into your course, the free handout for this book includes a job aid with more ideas and options for collaboration and teamwork in online courses.

Online Learner & Community Supports

Gunawardena et al. (2019) identified different types of support infrastructure that help an online learning community thrive. Much of this can easily be standard information and support that is integrated across multiple classes, so you are not the sole person developing and providing the supports. One helpful activity would be to work with your fellow teachers, school leadership, and support staff to map out the available forms of support and to integrate clear access to support structures into every class. The following checklist could be converted into an aid for gathering helpful information. By building into your class links to other resources and sup-

port people, you enable your learners to tap into the same support network
they would have if they were in the building.

- ❏ **Teacher/facilitator support:** This includes peers, instructors, and
  perhaps community experts as well as any mentors or coaches typically involved in the process.
- ❏ **Learning support:** This includes the communications mechanisms
  you will use, purposeful integration of regular and consistent feedback, links to resources, orientations, and other information and
  plans that directly support learning.
- ❏ **Technical support:** Make sure your students have quick and easy
  access to technical support contacts, 24-hour help desks, FAQs, help
  forums, and orientations. Often, this information gets sent out in
  myriad emails, and it's easy to lose track of. Keep everything organized for your learners and their caretakers by having a dedicated
  section in your course to keep all this information in a single spot.
- ❏ **Advisors/counselors:** Include contact information for academic
  advisers, counselors, and other support personnel at your school.
- ❏ **Libraries and databases:** Work with your librarians to create a module or section with information or tutorials that can be added to
  classes with links to the library, integrate library resources into your
  course, and add other links as appropriate. Librarians often have rich
  resources not just on locating materials but also on citation formats,
  paraphrasing, summarizing, and other important topics. Collaborat-

ing with your librarians can be a huge source of support for you as well as your students.

- ❏ **Institutional support:** Students or their caretakers often have questions about various procedural matters, policies, and other resources. If it doesn't exist already, work with your school leadership or staff to create an online information repository that you can link to from every class so you can easily direct students or caretakers to it when questions arise.
- ❏ **Regional centers:** Sometimes you may want to connect to a regional center that offers additional services, resources, or other courses or that is a good source for access to the internet or computers or that can provide training (e.g., software, typing, other types of training).

By creating bridges to these various sources of support, you help your learners connect not just to your class community but also into the larger educational support community—and this is essential to their success as online learners, to helping them feel supported, to building their confidence that they can manage any challenges and stress, and also to decreasing their sense of isolation.

Connections to SEL Teaching Practices

The teaching practices for SEL identified by Yoder (2014) discussed in this chapter as they are practiced in online teaching include:

Student-Centered Discipline

Once again, many of the strategies discussed in this chapter can help with online classroom management, such as establishing routines, setting course rules and expectations, and creating a community of support. For both SEL and for developing an online community, developing trust is essential. Student-centered discipline helps build a culture of trust and reciprocity, which are essential to a sense of community.

Warmth and Support

The community-building strategies in this chapter can help create a learning environment that is warm and supportive. The CoI Framework places particular emphasis on the belief that learning is a social process, not merely a matter of mastering concepts and ideas on one's own, and as such emphasizes creating a learning environment that nourishes important relationships in the learning process.

Cooperative Learning

How to support cooperation and collaboration and how to facilitate both in online education was covered in this chapter. Cooperative learning is even more impactful in an online environment than in the classroom because it helps learners connect with peers and not feel so isolated.

Classroom Discussions

Once again, I want to underscore the importance of classroom discussions and how you can use these to create a supportive climate in your online class. Encouragement and social presence cues, as well as more expressively communicating emotions online, help create a welcoming learning environment that fosters trust. This in turn makes students more willing to engage with the content and interact with others, which supports their learning, and discussions create a great opportunity for you to model for your students how to do this.

Competence Building—Modeling, Practicing, Feedback, Coaching

I touched a little bit on competence building in this chapter, specifically on modeling social presence cues and how to interact online in a healthy way. In the next chapter, I will explain in depth a framework that starts with modeling and builds on that for a robust metastrategy for online courses.

Summary

One of the reasons you may hear competing ideas around online learning is because there are two major philosophies that inform different approaches to online learning: individualized instruction and social learning theories. Educators who want to emphasize interactions and community will want to use a social learning approach for designing online learning. The Community of Inquiry framework is a time-tested social-learning framework for online learning that can help you generate ideas for how to make online learning more social and supportive. As part of this framework, you create social presence, cognitive presence, and teacher presence. These overlap to suggest strategies that support discourse, set the climate for your course, and help learners regulate their learning.

Strategies for creating community online include beginning in Week 1 with community building activities, like introductions, and activities or features you can maintain throughout the course, like the cyber café, a dedicated community space, peer support groups, and regular time and permission for students to socialize. Create a sharing time, create a sharing space, and cocreate this space with students so they can make it theirs and feel a sense of ownership of it. Teamwork—specifically cooperation and collaboration—is also a good strategy to employ online. Perhaps there are some opportunities in your course for students to work together on projects or to support each other as they develop their own projects. Collaboration can occur synchronously, during live class sessions, and asynchronously or a mix of both. Finally, keep in mind that what ultimately supports learners in their educational process is an entire ecosystem of support. Identify various aspects of that support system that students might otherwise have access to, and create access and links to those resources and supports in and through your class.

Assessment and Competency-Building Practices Online

The decisions you make around assessing learning have some of the most profound effects on your class learning culture. Ideally, as an educator wanting to develop SEL competencies in your learners, you want to build a community of trust with your students. A lot of hard-won progress can come crashing down, however, due to ill-fated assessment decisions. Unfortunately, educators witnessed the emergence of a lot of bad practices in spring and fall 2020, as schools rushed to implement plans for online learning. In particular, issues emerged around the use of proctoring software, which is software used to monitor students eye movement and behavior via their video cameras while they are taking a test or completing work at home.

How Assessment Contributes to Class Culture

Proctoring software can have an adverse effect on students' motivation, self-efficacy, and stress levels, and it can also create a strong culture of distrust between instructors and students. During 2020, students shared many instances, via social media, of software falsely detecting "cheating" behaviors when the student did not have full control of their home environment or when their lip movements, as they read questions out loud, were interpreted as talking or when eye movements—such as looking up to think or glancing at a clock on the desk—were interpreted as cheating by looking elsewhere for answers. Please be aware that the impact of these software packages on student learning, including social and emotional impacts, are largely untested and typically do not take diversity into account. Often, these programs penalize students with the greatest needs the most, and there is a disturbing pattern of discrimination emerging around this particular type of software. For example, some of them detect loud noises and flag this as problematic, so any learner who is at home in an environment with noises and others around them will be disproportionately affected. Swauger (2020) documents a range of issues with proctoring in higher education that are directly relevant to K–12 use as well. Issues he highlights include racial bias in the software (a lot of facial recognition algorithms used for online proctoring software are based on white skin and have major reliability issues), the long history of gender bias that underlies the technology used for proctoring software, and biases against neurodivergent learners, such as learners with ADHD.

In addition to the significant diversity and equity concerns about such software, numerous students and educators have raised concerns that it may violate students' privacy rights. Before procuring such software, you may want to convene a working group that involves all stakeholders, including parents and students, to investigate the software more carefully and to examine any potential legal and ethical issues, and to request policy guidance from your district or state.

In his book, *Cheating Lessons*, Lang (2013) discusses what leads to increased cheating as well as learning culture features that create conditions for cheating and features that decrease cheating—and, as a double bonus, that also have a positive impact on learning. Conditions that are more favorable to cheating include:

- Strong emphasis on a single outcome or a limited number of outcomes, such as one test or paper or just a few tests/papers
- Extremely high stakes—a lot is riding on few performances
- Extrinsic motivation—there is a reward or threat of punishment associated with performance rather than the joy of learning or improving, what Lang describes as a focus on what happens after the performance rather than the performance itself
- Low self-efficacy—learners lack confidence in their ability to complete a task successfully

Since trust and well-being are essential to positive learning outcomes and help us model the very sorts of SEL outcomes we wish to engender with our students, creating a learning environment that communicates trust is essential. Unlike the practices listed above, the following practices help create conditions that support learning instead of cheating:

- Emphasize mastery of learning and the learning process, including improvement over time, rather than performance at a fixed point in time.
- Create lower, more frequent stakes throughout the class (though, take care to avoid "death by a thousand cuts" from too many small-point items).
- Help learners develop higher self-efficacy by using authentic assessments and real problems that are more relevant to the real world, and provide them on-going strategy-focused feedback to help them develop confidence.
- Foster intrinsic motivation by placing more emphasis on the learning process and providing students strategy-focused feedback with opportunity to apply and improve over time.

While summative assessments are important, they should be well-balanced with meaningful formative assessments that are made throughout the course to provide students multiple opportunities to demonstrate their understanding and application, to receive constructive feedback, and to apply feedback to future learning and work (see Figure 5.1). This will help create a learning culture of trust in your online class because learners will understand that assessment is being used to help them in their learning process rather than as a form of behavior management or behavior/environmental policing. It also helps them develop their own ability to manage their learning process and manage their own behavior and environments.

FIGURE 5.1 Formative assessment integrated through the course

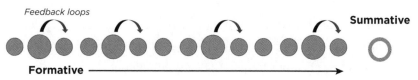

Feedback loops   **Summative**

Formative
Assessment for learning – informs the student's learning process
Provides strategy-focused feedback on what to improve
Can be used as a diagnostic as well or for progress monitoring

| Increases transfer of learning (active knowledge instead of inert knowledge) | Increases social presence, decreases sense of distance leads to ↓ Increased student satisfaction | Addresses issues with motivation (confidence) |

Consider how giving your students agency and autonomy can inform your assessment decisions.

Assessment of Learning Online

Teachers often have questions about *how* to assess online. The first thoughts that comes to mind are usually tests and quizzes because these are so easy to implement in an online class. However, quizzes and tests only assess basic knowledge or understanding, leaving a whole universe of other types of learning, and therefore other types of assessment, to explore. That universe affords particularly rich options for SEL, and you may even pick up some ideas here you want to use in your room-based class as well.

Online Assessment Methods

It is worth dedicating some discussion to assessment of learning in online environments. There are excellent opportunities to engage in meaningful assessment of online learning that move beyond tests and quizzes. Too often, assessment is used more as a monitoring strategy, and this assessment choice has led to invasive practices that harm students' trust in educators. Tools and policies that require students to show you everything in their physical space at home, for example, raise significant ethical concerns around student rights and privacy as well as questions about how such recordings and data are stored and maintained and how students can exercise their rights over their own data and environment. Assessment practices are a major leverage point for building—or eroding—trust and community and communicate social and emotional messages to your students about how you view them and what level of trust you have in them, and how much control they are given in regulating their own space and data.

Tests and quizzes are overused assessment methods, and quite often their use is not appropriately aligned with the learning objectives and outcomes. One way to mitigate issues around tests and quizzes is to limit the use of them to instances in which you are truly trying to measure basic retention or recall of content. For all other types of learning, use different assessment methods. Table 5.1 summarizes a range of options for how to assess online learning for the type of learning you wish to assess (based on Stiggins & Conklin, 1992 and Chappuis & Stiggins, 2016):

TABLE 5.1 Online Assessment Methods Based on Type of Learning

KNOWLEDGE	REASONING	SKILLS	PRODUCTS	DISPOSITIONS
Facts and concepts we want students to know	Students use what they know to reason and solve problems	Students use their knowledge and reasoning to perform a task skillfully	Students use their knowledge, reasoning, and skills to create a concrete product	Students' attitudes and beliefs about a given domain or expectations
Selected response	*Constructed or extended response*	*Performance assessment or demonstration*	*Product*	*Personal communications*
Examples for online use:				

Quiz or test tools (objective items) Audio voice threads (e.g., language instruction) Recitations (record something that must be memorized)	Open-ended quiz or test Sorting activities Record solving a problem and submit Present on a topic (live or recorded) Case studies that require students to apply content to derive the solution	Record a video performing a skill (e.g., a lab, an exercise routine, a talk-aloud on their design process for a product); assess with a rubric Perform a skill during a live video session (e.g., labs); assess with a rubric Simulation or role-playing	Complete a project—individually or as a group; assess with a rubric Construct a writing sample—individually or together—on a wiki or Google Doc (e.g., mimic a writer's style or revise an essay with issues that you load for them)	Maintain a reflection journal throughout class, with prompts that focus on learning strategies, beliefs, and/or attitudes Personal communi-cations—open questions during instruction, oral exams, one-on-one feedback loops

Assessing SEL Online

We could rename all of these to SEL Knowledge, SEL Reasoning, SEL Skills, and SEL Dispositions (maybe even SEL Products!). Table 5.2 has some examples of how you could assess different SEL objectives (from Chapter 1) online.

TABLE 5.2 SEL Standards and Possible Assessment Strategies

SEL STANDARD	ASSESSMENT STRATEGY
Individual demonstrates an understanding of their emotions.	• Observation students during whole-class and small-group time • Students maintain a weekly journal, using a blog or a journaling tool in the LMS, to submit personal reflections • Students submit a periodic video of themself talking about difficult emotions, like frustration or anger
Individual demonstrates knowledge of personal strengths, challenges, cultural and/or linguistic assets, and aspirations.	• Students create a "Map of Me" (concept map), mapping out their strengths, challenges, etc., on the computer or they draw it on paper and submit a photo of it or a video of them talking through it. You could have them do this project near the beginning of the year, then again in the middle of the year, and once more near the end of the year, as an on-going reflective activity.

Individual demonstrates the skills to manage and express their emotions, thoughts, impulses, and stress in constructive ways.	• Ask students to generate strategies they can use, either as a whole-class or as a small-group activity. Turn this into a self-assessment activity you use throughout the course, and have students self-assess areas of strength and areas to work on. You could also use this to frame observations of students during class interactions in order to provide feedback that is anchored in student-generated ideas.
Individual recognizes leadership capacity in themself and others.	• For any collaborative or cooperative/teamwork activities, have students write out their strengths and others' strengths. Have the groups produce a "Strengths Map" together for their group, either in a Google tool or a tool like Padlet, and submit it as a product.

Individual demonstrates skills to respectfully engage in and resolve interpersonal conflicts in various contexts.	• Create a series of role-playing simulations for students where they must resolve an interpersonal conflict. Having a series of these makes it possible for them to change roles. Observe how they work to resolve conflict, and provide scaffolding (e.g., prompts they can refer to for strategies or words they can use), strategy-focused feedback to help them grow, and opportunities to demonstrate growth. • Create a series of case studies reflecting interpersonal conflicts that students read and respond to on their own time, wherein students write or record a video explaining how they would handle it (individually or as a group) as well as a self-reflection on how well they think they would handle it and what they see as areas for growth. You could disseminate these case studies throughout the school year to provide continual opportunities to learn, reflect, and grow.

Self-Assessment

Time and again, we see that helping learners develop self-assessment is a critical strategy that is a hallmark of SEL teaching practices, and effective teaching practices in general, both in a classroom and online. Many of the examples provided above can be used to scaffold self-assessment, depending on how you choose to use them in your classroom.

Self-assessment is the ability to assess one's own learning. Wiggins and McTighe (2005), in their framework in *Understanding by Design*, expanded assessment to include self-knowledge—the ability to self-examine, self-reflect, self-evaluate, and express reflective insight. Learning self-regulation often helps with this, so many of the strategies discussed in Chapter 1 can help learners develop their self-assessment skills. By identifying opportunities for students to reflect on what they have learned, their process, what is working, and how to improve, teachers help them develop self-assessment skills. Blogs and online journals can be good tools for students to submit their reflections. Some students may prefer to submit videos of their reflections. Below are some general questions you could adapt to your students and specific class activities:

- What are the areas I want feedback on for this assignment/activity?
- How would I assess myself using the SEL standards? What are my strengths and which areas can I work on?
- Pick a particular area from SEL standards to focus on. What are some strategies you can use this week to improve in this area?
- What is helpful feedback? What attitudes and strategies are helpful when providing feedback to others?

You could also use quiz/testing tools in your LMS to provide students regular-but-quick self-assessments wherein they rate themselves on how they are doing in relation to SEL objectives and managing the class expectations. In one of my classes, which is one students typically take as their first online class, I have self-assessment quizzes that students take 4 times throughout the course that help facilitate self-reflection and self-assessment around being an online learner. A sampling of different types of self-reflection and self-assessment questions you can use or adapt are available at the back of the book and as a free handout. These may help you generate ideas for your own class. You might have students select responses that are descriptive or that indicate their self-assessment or confidence on a Likert-type scale (e.g., from 1 to 5); whatever you think would work best for your learners. Questions like these can help you communicate ideas and scaffold for students things they may not have thought about yet. In a number of these example questions I am restating SEL standards or using areas of self-regulation as self-reflection prompts.

Rubrics

Rubrics have a host of benefits that can be especially helpful in the online environment. You may often think of rubrics as providing structure for grading, but a well-developed rubric is even more valuable at the front end of the assignment and throughout the process. As you develop a rubric for an assignment, incorporate language that is strategy-focused and clearly tells students what you are looking for rather than language that focuses on errors. When I develop my rubrics, I try to develop them as if the rubric itself can provide immediate feedback to students.

You may also want to involve your class in the process of developing the rubric for the assignment, which is usually more effective later in the course rather than at the beginning of a school year. For example, after walking my writing and composition students through several rounds of editing earlier in the school year, I asked them to generate a list of what features and problem spots to look for in advance of a peer review session. Rather than me telling them what to look for, they identified the features, which I recorded in a Google Doc that the entire class had access to. Once we were done creating the list, I sent them into breakout rooms for active work during class using peer review—the groups had access to the Google Doc while they were in their small groups. From that point in class forward, every peer review session would begin with a whole-class exercise of generating expectations and problem areas, and then they would break into small groups for peer review. This gives learners choice and responsibility and helps them develop self-assessment skills.

Also consider how you can use rubrics throughout an assignment process—beginning, middle, and end—as instructional scaffolding, not just at the end for evaluation. In one of my classes in which we have a complex project, I devote part of a session to talking through the project rubric and how to use it. We discuss the project requirements and expectations. Then, while students are working on the project, I have some discussion forums where they share their projects in small groups and provide each other feedback on their projects using the rubric as a structure for feedback. This helps reinforce the expectations and supports students in developing self-assessment skills because the rubric is now not just the teacher's tool but also the learners' tool for improvement.

Competence Building—
The Cognitive–Affective Apprenticeship Model

Thus far, I have covered a range of practices and strategies. One robust metastrategy that can help pull everything together is the cognitive apprenticeship (CA) model (Brown & Palincsar, 1989), which for SEL is more appropriately called the cognitive–affective apprenticeship (CAA) model. The original cognitive apprenticeship model was developed as a process to teach complex problem solving and reasoning skills to novice learners with a sole focus on cognitive development. SEL standards are a mix of the cognitive domain (understanding, comprehension, and skill development) as well as the affective domain (receiving/attending, responding, valuing, internalizing values). The teaching methods in the apprenticeship model are useful for both types of objectives, and research has shown that this approach has a positive impact both on academic achievement as well as social and emotional development (Jekielek et al., 2002).

Teaching Methods for Building Competence

One of the things I like about the CAA model is that it is all about showing and guiding, not just telling. It also incorporates important elements that teachers may forget about but that are essential for reinforcement of learning and transfer of learning beyond the classroom environment. Sometimes I hear teachers refer to "I do—We do—You do," and this is a nice summary of the first three methods in the CAA model, but not all of them, and the last three methods are essential. There are six teaching methods that are part of this model and that help learners develop cognitive, affective, and metacognitive strategies (Collins et al., 1987; Brown et al., 1989). Think of these not as different methods to choose from but as a methodological process wherein each method is used systematically to facilitate the learning process. I commonly refer to it as a metastrategy because it is a strategy for instructional strategies. And you can apply this metastrategy at the lesson, unit, and class levels; it is a very flexible model.

TEACHING METHODS	EXAMPLES
Modeling	*Modeling is a form of direct instruction (a presentation strategy).* Demonstrate the desired skills and attributes Create opportunities for students to observe one or more experts Modeling is possible in-person and through 3D animations, recorded video, or live video

TEACHING METHODS	EXAMPLES
Coaching	*Coaching is a type of strategy-focused feed-back you can use as part of your formative assessment plan.* Create opportunity for students to practice their application of the knowledge and skills (in this case, SEL objectives) Observe the student demonstrating a competency/skill Provide individualized, strategy-focused feed-back to students (anchored in the checklist/rubric/another support) Use dialogue with students that is facilitative, not directive

TEACHING METHODS	EXAMPLES
Scaffolding	*Scaffolding takes the shape of resources, supports, and hints you provide learners so they can work increasingly independently.* Help students create conceptual models/ remember processes Articulate heuristics or rules of thumb that can be easily remembered Provide students hints, reminders, or suggestions Provide students a checklist, rubric, or another sort of performance support (e.g., could be a picture list for younger learners) to refer to both during practice and later on their own Support students with access to important resources

TEACHING METHODS	EXAMPLES
Articulation	*Articulation is a form of both formative and summative assessment. It can also be used for self-assessment to help develop meta-cognition. This is an oft overlooked step in the process.* Support students with dialogue—ask them questions that spur them to explain their rationale or their process Ask students to explain their thinking and process as they are working (formative) as well as after they have completed an activity or product (summative) Provide feedback on their thinking and process as they are working (formative) as well as after they have completed the activity or product (summative)

TEACHING METHODS	EXAMPLES
Reflection	*Reflection, a commonly overlooked step, is a form of self-assessment that can help develop metacognition.* Include opportunities for students to reflect on their performance after-the-fact—intentionally incorporate reflection discussions, activities, or assignments Facilitate a compare-and-contrast process so learners can think about how they handled a scenario or solved a problem as compared to someone with more experience Provide students encouragement in their process
Exploration	*Exploration is a form of application or "transfer" of learning—students take what they have learned and apply it to a new area.* Encourage students to identify other situations or problems they can work through Prompt students to ask more questions and update their models/process/checklist Provide students an opportunity to exercise their newly developed skills and process with less direction and scaffolding (or using the same scaffolding you already provided)

Sequencing

A good way to implement the CAA model is to go through the process several times throughout your class and use sequencing strategies to develop competencies in increasingly more complex situations (Brown, 1985; Lave, 1990; VanLehn and Brown, 1980; White, 1984). Three specific sequencing strategies can be helpful for planning:

- **Sequence to increasing complexity:** Sequence tasks to gradually increase in difficulty.
- **Sequence to increasing diversity:** Allow students to practice in a variety of situations to help them develop broader application of their knowledge and skills.
- **Sequence from global to local skills:** Start with explaining the whole task, then break it down into parts that they can connect back to the whole.

As you sequence students from less difficult to more difficult examples, you want to slowly fade away the scaffolding so they are increasingly independent in their process. In practice, this could take the shape of activities and scenarios you have students work and talk through on a regular basis (e.g., weekly, every other week, monthly), wherein you start them with simpler situations or simpler forms of situations and then ask them to take on increasingly difficult example scenarios or situations as

FIGURE 5.2 Sequencing With the Apprenticeship Model

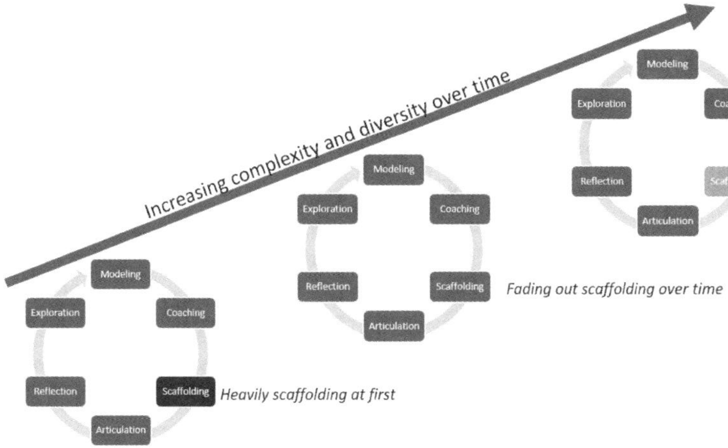

well as a range of different situations. This approach can also help you adapt to new situations or needs that may arise; if something happens in class or outside of class, you could readily adapt an existing time slot to focus on a timely situation or problem. As you work through activities, scenarios, or situations, you follow the same process every time of modeling, coaching, scaffolding, articulation, reflection, and exploration (see Figure 5.2).

Let's walk through some ideas and examples of how you can do this online.

TEACHING METHODS	EXAMPLES
Modeling	There are a variety of ways you can model an approach for students: Tell a story (recorded or wlive) about a time when you were dealing with a difficult situation and how you handled it. Write or record a scenario or case study for your students, then either recorded or during a live class session, talk out loud through the questions you would ask, how you would handle the situation, and what you are thinking. Ask others to record authentic stories and share them. Hearing from older peers can make it more personal and relevant. One good strategy may be to ask older students at your school, or previous students of yours, to share a story. Either they could record and send it to you or you could record an interview with them and then share it with your class. Pick a book to read either outside of class or during the live session that models decision making and problem solving, then discuss as a class how the character(s) handled the situation. Talk-alouds are a great way of modeling a thought or problem-solving process.

TEACHING METHODS	EXAMPLES
Coaching	There are a variety of ways you can provide coaching for students. The key here is for students to start doing on their own while you provide them feedback:
	Give students a scenario and have them work through it on their own or in small groups during your live class session. As they do, use coaching questions to guide the discussion (see below, adapted from Stone & Heen's book *Thanks for the Feedback*).
	Provide students a written scenario or a recorded video that describes or depicts a scenario, then ask them to describe how they would resolve the situation. They could either write a response or record themselves talking through their decision-making and problem-solving.
	You could discuss submissions with them using coaching questions through feedback on what they submitted or as part of a whole-class or small-group discussions during a live session.
	You could also replay a recorded performance that you annotate with audio comments, written comments, or both.
	A role-playing simulation can also be a great strategy for coaching. Put students in pairs or small groups, and assign them specific roles. This gives students an opportunity for practice while you observe and ask coaching questions to support their process. You can have them role-play during a live class session, which works well for all age groups, or older students could meet independently and record their simulation and submit the recording to you.

TEACHING METHODS	EXAMPLES			
	Clarifying Questions "I'm interested in hearing more about . . ." "Based on your experience . . ." "Tell me how . . ."	*Observational Questions* "I noticed how when you _____, that _____."	*Exploring Questions* "What might it sound like or look like to _____?" "What ideas/ strategies/ process might you use to _____?"	*Catalytic Questions* "It sounds like you are not so happy or clear about _____. What would you like to do differently next time? "It seems like you are considering _____. Can you explain?"
Coaching				

TEACHING METHODS	EXAMPLES
Scaffolding	There are a variety of ways you can provide scaffolding for students online: You could provide students with a conceptual model or process, or you could have an activity where students think through a model or process and you develop that as a class or in small groups. In some instances, you may want to provide students with a rule of thumb or checklist, and in other instances (e.g., with older students) you might do an activity where you develop a checklist, hints, reminders, or other resources or supports together. If you do this, you will want to circle back later to discuss any updates or modifications. Make resources easily accessible online or in a format that students can download and use. Ideally, create this in a flexible format that students can either print and write on or fill in on the computer. Provide students with a summary document or a site with support tools and links to resources that they can download and save to use, even after the year is done.

TEACHING METHODS	EXAMPLES
Articulation	There are a variety of ways students could provide articulation: In addition to submitting a recording of how they would solve the problem, have them either record or write a companion piece in which they explain their rationale and approach/process. Ask students to maintain a journal or blog throughout the course, that is shared only with you, in which they explain their rationale and approach for each activity or scenario. You could also use this to have them reflect on real situations they are encountering as well as how they are applying what they're learning from these activities to real situations. Most LMSs have a blog or journal tool, and Google Docs can also work well for this. Use the coaching questions (above) during a live class session with students, in small-groups, or in one-on-one conference sessions to prompt meaningful articulation in real time and provide opportunities for feedback.

TEACHING METHODS	EXAMPLES
Reflection	There are different ways you can engage students in reflection online: Synchronous comparison: One great option for reflection is to invite an expert (could be an older student) to give a guest talk in your live class about how they handled a situation similar to what your students just finished working through. Then ask students to compare and contrast how they handled the scenario to how the guest expert handled it and to identify strategies they could use in the future. Asynchronous comparison: If it makes more sense to do this asynchronously, you can present the modeling video, then give students an activity to complete (asynchronous coaching with scaffolding), after which they watch a recorded video by someone with more experience talking about how they would handle that scenario or how they did handle a similar situation. Follow that with another activity in which students submit a written or recorded think-aloud comparing and contrasting and identifying strategies they could use in the future. Post-hoc reflection: Have students submit a written or recorded reflection using video, audio, a journal or blog tool, or simply a document in which they reflect on how they can improve next time. Discussion: A discussion forum or a live class discussion (whole-class or small-group) can also be a good place to reflect on one's own performance and learn from other's reflections. You could use some of these strategies simultaneously so students have an opportunity to hear and learn from others but also to share personal insights in a safe way that only you would read or hear.

TEACHING METHODS	EXAMPLES
Exploration	There are a number of ways you can create opportunities for exploration online: Periodically allocate some time, either during live class sessions or in discussion forums, for students to generate specific problem spaces or situations for exploration. You could identify specific times when this will occur and, at each time, assign 3 or 4 students to pick a scenario or problem to tackle and, perhaps, to lead the discussion. Talk students through the process of identifying who might be an expert and which resources might be good to consult in order to learn more. They could interview someone in a video conferencing tool and record that interview to share, create resources together that they share, etc. You may want to obtain permission forms for the students to have the experts sign, preferably vetted by your school or district counsel. Walk students through an activity as a whole-class or in small groups in which you generate new/additional questions. If you worked together as a group to generate a conceptual model, rubric, checklist, or other performance support tool, revisit that and update it together.

The following are some scenarios that are particularly relevant to online learning and that may help jog some ideas for your class. You may want to flesh these out more and incorporate descriptions or details that are more specific to your class or context.

- There are a lot of noises or distractions in my learning environment at home.
    - What are the feelings I'm feeling about the distractions around me?
    - What are some strategies I can use to help me manage my feelings?
    - What are some strategies I can use to help me manage what I can control in my learning environment at home?
    - What solutions have I come up with for managing distractions at home that I could share with your classmates?

- I miss seeing my friends/my teacher(s) at school.
    - What are the feelings you are feeling about this?
    - What are some strategies I can use to help me manage my feelings?
    - What solutions have I, or others, come up with for managing this that I could share?

- I feel like others talk over me or ignore me and as if I don't get to share or have a say in class.
    - What are the feelings I am feeling about this?
    - What are some strategies I can use to help me manage my feelings?
    - What solutions have I, or others, come up with for managing this that I could share?

- I have a very hard time concentrating and/or I feel overwhelmed by having to study and learn at home instead of at school.
    - What am I feeling about the distractions around me?
    - What are some strategies I can use to help me manage my feelings?
    - What are some strategies I can use to help me manage what I can control in my learning environment at home?
    - What solutions have I come up with for managing distractions at home that I could share with classmates?

- There are a lot of changes happening right now at school, at home, and in the world, and I am feeling stressed by them.
    - What are the feelings I'm feeling about this?
    - What are some strategies I can use to help me manage my feelings?
    - What solutions have I, or others, come up with for managing distractions at home that I could share with classmates?
    - How would I advise a friend if a friend reached out to me saying they felt stressed about all these changes?

Some general topics for discussion may be helpful:

- A friend asks you to let them copy your homework.
    - How does this make you feel?
    - What process can you use to decide what to do?

- Using your process, what would you decide to do?
- How can you communicate your decision to your friend?

- You have a big test in a class next week.
  - How are you feeling about the test? What are your positive feelings about the test? What are your negative feelings about the test?
  - How accurate are your negative feelings? What evidence do you have that you will do fine on the test?
  - What strategies can you use to help you prepare for the test?
  - How can you manage your time well to prepare well?

- You get frustrated if your work is not perfect/not good enough.
  - How do you feel when you make a mistake or find a mistake in your work?
  - What goes through your mind when you find or make a mistake?
  - What evidence do you have around you that you are doing a good job and that your work *is* good enough? For example, what feedback are you receiving from your teacher or others?
  - What are some things you can say to yourself about your work when you find or make a mistake?
  - When might it be important to have high expectations, and when might it be okay if your work is not absolutely perfect?

Connection to SEL Teaching Practices

Let's connect the ideas I have covered in this chapter to general SEL teaching practices identified by Yoder (2014).

Classroom Discussions

As you may have already gathered, classroom discussions are a cornerstone practice for online instruction. This is where the discussions around content happen, where you can observe students immediately, in synchronous discussions or see how well they can integrate and elaborate in an asynchronous discussion. Using both of these modalities will help students with different types of communication skills—verbal and written—and affords you opportunities to model communication skills as well. These are great practice areas not just for academic content but for SEL content as well, and these practice areas align particularly well with the teaching methods in the cognitive–affective apprenticeship model.

Self-Reflection and Self-Assessment

These teaching practices involve explicitly asking your students to actively think about their work. Providing students with a few questions or prompts, along with examples of questions they can use to self-assess, and some time for them to reflect can help them stop to process everything they are learning and digest it cognitively and psychologically. The Rubrics and Self-Assessment subsections in this chapter provided ideas for how to facilitate this online.

Academic Press and Expectations

"Academic press" means using appropriately challenging work to press or stretch students, and academic "expectations" are your beliefs that all students can succeed. Students know when you believe in them through your behaviors, not just your words. By providing your students with challenges and by making it clear that you believe each of them can meet the challenges, your confidence in the students transfers to them and bolsters their motivation to learn and tackle the challenges you lay out for them. This involves knowing how your students are performing and anticipating their emotional responses to challenges so you can help them manage those responses. One thing I commonly hear from teachers who have taught online is that they feel they get to know their students—including their work and their capabilities—better and can provide better feedback that is truly tailored to each student. Whereas feedback provided on assignments handed back in a classroom can produce a sense of distance, feedback provided on online assignments can come across as more conversational, especially if you incorporate feedback as a formative assessment strategy, which allows students to iterate on their work. Both sections on assessment strategies and the apprenticeship model in this chapter provide specifics on how you can use challenging work to press or stretch students while at the same time building their confidence, motivating them, and making the learning explicit.

Competence Building—
Modeling, Practicing, Feedback, Coaching

Students build SEL competencies when teachers provide systematic instruction through clear objectives, introduction of materials, modeling, practice, and reflection. In Chapter 1, I talked about SAFE practices and the importance of having clear objectives and instructional strategies, activities, and assessments that are aligned with those objectives. The model explored in this chapter can help us pull this together.

Summary

Your assessment strategies can have a significant impact on your class culture. With online education in particular, it may be tempting to use tests and quizzes because the tools are readily available, but you should select the assessment method that's right for the type of learning you want to assess. For SEL competencies, you can use a range of assessment methods for reasoning, demonstrating skills, analysis, and evaluation that are much better suited to SEL standards and that provide a lot more opportunities for formative feedback and can support self-assessment as well. Developing rubrics that are a form of stand-alone support and guidance can help students develop self-assessment skills.

I have covered a lot of different strategies and ideas thus far, and one metastrategy you can use to pull it all together is the cognitive–affective apprenticeship model. This involves modeling, coaching, scaffolding, articulation, reflection, and exploration. You can apply this model during live (synchronous) class time, through asynchronous activities, or use a blend of both. Specific sequencing strategies are also helpful for scaffolding your students to advance from simpler to more complex problems or situations and allow practice across a variety of situations to help them develop broader application of their knowledge and skills. By starting with the whole task then breaking it down into parts, they can connect specific ideas or strategies back to big ideas.

Reflective Online Teaching

Because so few teachers had prior experience teaching online before spring 2020, a lot of learning has been taking place around our practices online since then. I want to close this book by focusing on reflective practices for online teaching and on ideas for transitioning between online and classroom environments with an eye towards future preparedness.

Reflective teaching has long been considered a cornerstone of effective teaching practices. In 1983, Donald Schön published *The Reflective Practitioner*, and hundreds of studies and books have been written on the topic since. Reflective practice is grounded in the idea that we are continually learning and improving, and Schön argued in a separate book, *Technology and Change* (1967), that modern life is marked by constant change, requiring continual reflection and learning—which certainly is true for the major changes we have all been through recently. Reflective practice is a way to respond positively to change and to exert agency in a situation in which you may feel you have had little. It includes learning from others as well as conducting self-assessments, it focuses on improving your professional practices, and it is something we do throughout our careers.

Reflective teaching is a subset of reflective practice. Most definitions of reflective teaching are grounded in assumptions that the teaching is taking place in a classroom. There are a lot of resources out there already on self-assessment of teaching to support reflection on your classroom pedagogy, identifying strengths, and identifying areas for revision or improvement. Next, I will discuss ways to adapt those practices to our online teaching and identify areas that are unique to online learning.

Self-Care While Teaching Online

Reflection and self-assessment are hard to engage in when you are tired and feeling stressed. Online teaching can be demanding and draining, even for those of us who have been teaching online for many years. Computer screens are hard on our eyes over time, and sitting at a desk all day can be hard on our bodies. In addition, educators have had criticism unfairly directed at them for various decisions around online learning, and many teachers have expressed deep angst over not being able to see and work with their most vulnerable learners in person. Self-care is an important foundation for reflective practice, so let's start with some self-care strategies that are particularly important for online teaching.

Take Brain Breaks and Physical Breaks

Teaching for a full day in-person is tiring, but, as you have no doubt discovered, teaching online can be even more tiring. This is doubly true when you are doing it for the first time, as there is also the added cognitive load of learning the systems, thinking your way through strategies, building course resources, etc. With little lead time for planning and development, all of that front-end planning and development can get compressed on top of actual implementation and delivery. It can also be easy to lose track of time. It is important to take breaks throughout the day—brain breaks and physical breaks. I wear a watch that buzzes me periodically, reminding me to stretch and stand or take a few quick steps. I also have switched to a desk arrangement where I can raise and lower the monitors and keyboard to go between standing and sitting. If that is feasible, you may find this helps you break up time spent sitting. There are pads you can use to stand on that provide support for your body as well as pads that allow you to balance or rock/move while you are standing. I personally like the rocking pads and find that having some small motion while I work helps me focus better and also keeps my body moving rather than just sitting. Whether it's popping into the kitchen for another drink, a few minutes outside in the sun for a reset, or a walk around the block, building in breaks that are both mental and physical throughout the day every day will improve your ability to catch your breath and reflect.

Build in Time for Everyone—Including You— to Work Away From the Computer

It isn't physically healthy for you or your students to work at the computer or be on a device all day long. I have twins whose experiences for part of kindergarten and all of first grade were fully online instruction during the pandemic. One of the strategies their school employed for kindergarten through third grade was intentionally limiting the amount of screen time to 1.5–2 hours per day and designing the rest of the day to be away from the screen or to have minimal screen time (e.g., do an activity or create something then take a picture or video and submit that). This is healthy for the students and healthy for you too. Plan your time so that your day includes intentional time away from the screen. I use the calendar in Outlook to create "me-time appointments" so that reminders will pop up and so that I do not plan class time or other meetings during that time. By chunking your time into smaller pieces of screen time and off-screen time throughout the day, you will lower the impact of using screens and too much sitting.

Use Mindfulness Strategies for Yourself

Many of the mindfulness practices and strategies in the other books in this series are ones you can use for yourself, not just for your students. For example, the focusing and breathing activities that I discussed earlier and that Jennings (2019) covers in her book are activities you can integrate into your own daily and weekly personal routine outside of class. I use quick breathing strategies throughout the day to take quick breaks or to gather my thoughts before a meeting that I think may be complicated. You may find it helpful to work through Jennings's book and create a personal plan for mindfulness so you can tend to yourself and better manage stresses.

These practices—taking breaks, allocating time away from the computer, and practicing mindfulness strategies—are important for reflection because they provide you the time, space, and opportunity to reflect. If you feel these tools are not sufficient, a resource that goes into more depth is Jennings's (2020) book, *Teacher Burnout Turnaround*. This could even be a good candidate for a virtual book club for you to go through with colleagues as you navigate pressures, changes, and frustrations.

While self-care strategies provide you some agency in areas you can control, one significant limitation of self-care strategies is that it places a focus on the individual. However, several decades' worth of workplace performance studies indicate that individual knowledge or skills account for 10–20% of performance. The rest of the variability—80–90%—is due to "systemic factors" (Triner et al., 1996). As Rummler and Brache stated, "if you pit a good performer against a bad system, the system will win almost every time" (1995, p. 13). In particular, the systemic barriers or supports that greatly influence workplace performance are: resources (or lack thereof), policies (which can be contradictory or run counter to spoken or unspoken expectations), job/task definitions and expectations (which may include unclear, changing, or unspoken expectations), rewards and incentives (or lack thereof), communications and feedback loops, motivation, and knowledge and skills (Watkins, 2007). In many studies of why a new idea doesn't work as envisioned, implementation issues do not stem from individuals who lack knowledge or skills but from lack of resources, problematic or absent policies, disincentives, poor communications or feedback loops, and issues with clarity around what is part of someone's job (and what is not).

In one example, a recent study of new teacher induction at 12 mid-size schools, Moore and Hoffman (2020) found that of all the barriers and supports identified for new teachers, resources accounted for 34% of the barriers mentioned, and communications and feedback loops accounted for 20% of barriers mentioned, with knowledge and skills accounting only for 14% of barriers mentioned. This finding is consistent with other research on workplace performance that helps highlight how educators and administrators need to tend to systemic barriers and supports, not place the burden on individuals to "fix themselves." These findings should not be misinterpreted to suggest that knowledge and skills (which are the only types of barrier or support that an individual has direct agency over) aren't important but that they are only part of the solution set, not the entirety. If it is within your power, you may want to conduct a needs/gap analysis using this sort of approach to identify what barriers you can remove and what supports you can reinforce to help teachers at your school get the sorts of supports they need. Jennings's book, *Teacher Burnout Turnaround*, provides a lot of strategies that focus more on systemic factors.

Reflective Teaching

One thing I commonly hear from teachers who are new to online education is that they learned a great deal through teaching online that they can apply to their classroom practices as well. While the 2020 changes forced many teachers to teach online under less-than-ideal circumstances, there are still several important insights to carry forward through reflective teaching. Reflective teaching includes both self-assessment and external assessment. Let's break this down into what you can assess and then how you can assess and reflect.

Most existing models for reflective teaching focus on reflections on your students, yourself, your pedagogy, your curriculum, and the school environment. These are all important, and you should continue to reflect on these areas as well, but for online learning you may feel like this is missing an important element or two: the online teaching environment and your home work environment. Let's extend the reflection process by incorporating specific questions related to online teaching and the new environments.

Student Learning

What does my data (hard and soft) say about what my students have learned?

Student Experience

What feedback am I receiving or detecting about students' experiences in the online setting?

What can I do to create a better online learning experience for my students?

What new practices are benefitting my students that I should consider continuing, regardless of whether we are online or in-person?

Online Strategies

What approaches am I not happy with? For example, if I want more interaction in my class, what strategies can I use to facilitate interaction?

Did activity X or Y work well? If not, why not, and what do I think I should do differently next time?

Online Teaching

What is working for me as an online teacher, and what is not working for me?

What are my strengths as an online teacher?

What are areas I could learn more about by talking with fellow teachers about how they handle or approach different things?

What new practices have I learned that I can continue to use regardless of whether we are online or in-person?

Work Environment

What is my best working environment for online teaching?

How can I minimize distractions?

What might make my work environment at home more comfortable or easier on my eyes/body or could put resources within easier reach?

You can gather information in different ways. While I have provided many ideas, I recommend that you keep your use of them to a minimum if this is your first year teaching online, as even just a few reflective strategies can generate a lot of action items. You may already know of things you want to improve, so using more extensive strategies may not help you generate new insights early on but may be more helpful once you have had some time to make those improvements. The following are some ideas for self-assessment and external assessment for reflective practice.

Self-Assessment for Reflection

- **Quick Notes:** The day is going to move quickly, so keep a notepad by you for quick notes or an open Google Doc on another screen where you can quickly jot down notes to help you recall details you may otherwise forget by the end of the day. I usually create a Google Doc and keep running notes throughout the course for improvements and ideas.

- **Reflection Journal:** A journal takes note taking a step further, in that you take time to write out what went well, what you weren't happy with, and what your action plan is. You may also wish to note how something made you feel to help you process your feelings, especially if a difficult situation arose during the day.

- **Video-Recorded Practices:** You may be recording your teaching online. This creates a good opportunity to go back through and watch your instruction to identify areas for improvement or to double check interactions and see what you may have missed or could address better next time. Many people do not like watching or hearing themselves, so this may be an uncomfortable strategy. If so, talk with a trusted colleague about sharing recordings and providing mutual feedback.

- **Teaching Portfolio:** This is time consuming and may be something you do after you've made your way through your first or second online teaching experience, but a teaching portfolio is a great way to pull together examples of your work, to demonstrate your strengths, and to write reflections on your practices.

External Assessment for Reflection

- **Peer Feedback:** Online learning is more transparent, making it easier for a trusted colleague to sit in on a session, view a recording, or tour your class site in the LMS. This can also be a great way to share ideas across grade-level teams or content-area teams. Be sure to keep the focus on coaching and constructive feedback rather than evaluative feedback.

- **Student Evaluations:** While you may have standard evaluation questions that go out to students, you can create your own questions for students that you send out periodically and/or at the end of the year. Some questions you can ask students include:
  - What did you find valuable in this unit?
  - What did you find difficult?
  - What were the top two or three things you learned?
  - Were there any activities or resources that you did not think were helpful?
  - What were the most helpful activities or resources?
  - Do you have suggestions on how I could improve this unit/lesson?
  - What advice would you give future students for this lesson/class?
  - If/when we move back to the classroom, what features of online teaching did you like and hope we keep?

Of course, gathering information and input is only useful if you put it to work. After you have taken the time to take notes, keep a journal, survey students, or employ the other strategies, be sure to take time periodically to write out your reflections more extensively and generate an action plan based on the data you've gathered and the insights you generate.

Finally, take stock not just of what to improve but of what is working well and what you are learning. Identify your metrics for success, not just learning outcomes, and continually remind yourself of the ways in which you and your students are succeeding. How are your actions helping keep students healthy, for example? How are you contributing to their well-being and their resilience? How are you creating a caring learning environment for them? How are you sending them the message that they matter? And how are you doing the same for yourself?

Looking Ahead—Transitioning Between Modalities

Chances are, a large number of teachers who have been teaching online will at some point move back into the classroom or may find themselves going between the classroom and the online environment for a while. Your reflective practices can help you prepare for these transitional times. Blended learning can be a great way for you to carry on the great, new practices you have learned from teaching online and to keep your class prepared for possible shifts back to online learning while also allowing you to leverage what's best about both learning environments.

One of the most common themes in research on technology across all different environments is that it's not the technology that has agency. Technology doesn't "cause" things to happen or "lead to" this or that. It is we humans who have the agency, and what happens is a direct result of the decisions we make around technology, from how it is designed to what is selected to how it is implemented. A question I get asked often is whether online learning is going to "take over" education, and my response is always that online learning isn't going to do anything that we don't decide for it to do. My goal all along has been to ensure that when we do use online education, we use it well. Looking ahead, past the pandemic that drove so many to teach online, what I hope will evolve is an educational ecosystem in which we more thoughtfully blend the possibilities of online and classroom-based teaching and learning.

If you recall the discussion on affordances that I started with, there are things that are better suited for online learning and things for which the classroom or face-to-face is better. Classroom environments may be better for providing students with resource-rich, distraction-free (or distraction-less) environments, especially for those with high needs or difficult home situations. But online environments are more effective for connecting with others who aren't in the same geographic location, for exploring environments that are physically impossible to access, and for working in a more distributed manner. Using online and classroom-based teaching together could also create new opportunities. For example, what if high school students could engage in activities at the school, for which it made sense to be on school grounds, during a part of the week or a part of the semester but could work at internships, co-ops, or other important real-life and adult-transitioning experiences that are off school grounds while watching recorded direct instruction and cooperating or collaborating through online team-based projects for the other portion of the time? What if middle schoolers could be provided flex-time to start exploring interest areas in their own time while also learning how to self-regulate better through opportunities that require and afford more self-regulation?

Within your own class, you can create more flexibility and create new opportunities as well by blending online interactions with classroom interactions. For social and emotional learning, there is great potential for you to provide supports and opportunities for your students not just in class but outside of class as well. For example, you might decide that you want to keep recorded mindfulness activities and self-reflection activities integrated into your class, such that students can complete them on their own at home or they have some they complete in class and some they can complete at home. An added benefit of doing this is it builds flexibility and adaptability into your class structure, so if the need arises to lean on online environments again, you already have it woven into the fabric of your class, and everyone can transition more smoothly to a fully online environment. You can engage your students in this reflective process by talking with them and/or surveying them about what would be helpful to keep from the online class and why (e.g., perhaps it provides them more flexibility or they like having access to resources on their own time in the evening).

Summary

Reflective teaching and self-assessment are important for mining insights from teaching in a new environment and continually improving your practice. Under stressful circumstances, this may require taking time for self-care as well, but be careful not to assume that self-care is a cure-all strategy.

Other systemic barriers and supports will likely require attention, such as adequate resources or supportive policies or healthy and timely communications and feedback loops.

Reflective teaching includes both self-assessment and external assessment. You can engage in self-assessment through activities like taking quick notes and journaling. For external assessment, peer reviews and student feedback can provide you with external input as to practices to keep and practices to improve or pitch.

On the heels of such a stressful year, during which many schools made the move to online education quickly and in many instances with little planning or support, this may seem like a chapter in your career that you're ready to put behind you. But there are a lot of new insights to be had that could benefit your students, such as providing them with more flexibility, more time for reflection and integration, or other types of benefits. If you plan to return to the classroom or teach in both online and class-based environments, identify practices that you may want to continue, wherein you leverage the online environment for the things it affords better even as you return to the classroom. Recently, one educator started a Twitter discussion using the hashtag #OnlineTeachingLove, and educators are sharing what they love about online teaching. For example, one contributor stated that online teaching provides an opportunity to think about how to convey content in new ways. Another teacher shared that she loves providing feedback to students and facilitating a space for peer feedback and online exchanges. Others shared how they loved learning more about their students and sharing silly videos and moments during class. Several mentioned how they felt online could be more personal and how virtual meetings felt more relaxed and were great opportunities to see each other in our homes with our kids and pets. Another mentioned how she uses technologies like Discord and blogs to get to know students more personally. One writing teacher shared that she loves teaching writing and communication asynchronously online because students can continuously practice the lessons and it provides a great opportunity for practicing effective multimodal communication.

Personally, I love teaching online because I feel like I get to know my students and their work better, I can provide them more direct support, and I really enjoy the flexibility afforded to both me and my learners. And I love the opportunities for deep reflection that tools like asynchronous discussions afford—students generate amazing work in these spaces, and that gives me such a great window into their thinking and learning. Teaching online has challenged me to rethink my teaching practices and helped me re-envision what the learning environment can look like, putting more emphasis on what can be afforded and how, erasing the walls around the classroom. For me, online teaching is like a canvas, full of so much creative potential, both on its own and blended with classroom teaching and learning, and limited only by my imagination. I hope you will similarly find joys, creative ideas, and new practices as you explore this creative space.

References

Abe, J. A. A. (2005). The predictive validity of the Five-Factor Model of personality with preschool age children. *Journal of Research in Personality, 39*(4), 423–442. https://doi.org/10.1016/j.jrp.2004.05.002

Abe, J. A. A. (2020). Big five, linguistic styles, and successful online learning. *The Internet and Higher Education, 45.* https://doi.org/10.1016/j.iheduc.2019.100724

Adams Becker, S., Cummins, M., Davis, A., Freeman, A., Hall Giesinger, C., & Ananthanarayanan, V. (2017). *NMC Horizon Report: 2017 higher education edition.* The New Media Consortium.

Alexander, B., Ashford-Rowe, K., Barajas-Murphy, N., Dobbin, G., Knott, J., McCormack, M., Pomerantz, J., Seilhamer, R., & Weber, N. (2019). EDUCAUSE Horizon Report: 2019 higher education edition. *LearnTechLib.* https://www.learntechlib.org/p/208644/

Aspen Institute. (2018). Pursuing social and emotional development through a racial equity lens: A call to action. *The Aspen Institute.* https://assets.aspeninstitute.org/content/uploads/2018/05/Aspen-Institute_Framing-Doc_Call-to-Action.pdf

Association for Supervision and Curriculum Development. (2007). *The learning compact redefined: A call to action—A report of the Commission on the Whole Child.* Retrieved October 17, 2020, from http://www.ascd.org/learningcompact

Bandura, A. (1989). Human agency in social cognitive theory. *American Psychologist*, *44*(9), 1175–1184. https://doi.org/10.1037/0003-066X.44.9.1175

Barbour, M. K., & Reeves, T. C. (2009). The reality of virtual schools: A review of the literature. *Computers & Education*, *52*(2), 402–416. https://doi.org/10.1016/j.compedu.2008.09.009

Bassani, P. (2011). Interpersonal exchanges in discussion forums: A study of learning communities in distance learning settings. *Computers & Education*, *56*(4), 931–938.

Beckett, K. (2019). Dewey online: A critical examination of the Communities of Inquiry approach to online discussions. *Philosophical Studies in Education*, *50*, 46–58.

Benson, P. L. (2006). *All kids are our kids: What communities must do to raise caring and responsible children and adolescents* (2nd ed.). Jossey-Bass.

Bernard, R., Abrami, P., Lou, Y., Borokhovski, E., Wade, A., Wozney, L., Wallet, P., Fiset M., & Huang, B. (2004). How does distance education compare to classroom instruction? A meta-analysis of the empirical literature. *Review of Educational Research*, *74*, 379–439.

Bidjerano, T., & Dai, D. Y. (2007). The relationship between the big-five model of personality and self-regulated learning strategies. *Learning and Individual Differences*, *17*(1), 69–81. https://doi.org/10.1016/j.lindif.2007.02.001

Blank, G., & Reisdorf, B. C. (2012). The participatory web: A user perspective on Web 2.0. *Information, Communication & Society*, *15*(4), 537–554. https://doi.org/10.1080/1369118X.2012.665935

Blau, I. (2011). E-collaboration within, between, and without institutions: Towards better functioning of online groups through networks. *International Journal of e-Collaboration, 7*(4), 22–36. https://doi.org/10.4018/jec.2011100102

Blau, I., & Shamir-Inbal, T. (2017). Re-designed flipped learning model in an academic course: The role of co-creation and co-regulation. *Computers & Education*, *115*, 69–81. https://doi.org/10.1016/j.compedu.2017.07.014

Blau, I., Shamir-Inbal, T., & Avdiel, O. (2020). How does the pedagogical design of a technology-enhanced collaborative academic course promote digital literacies, self-regulation, and perceived learning of students? *The Internet and Higher Education*, *45*. https://doi.org/10.1016/j.iheduc.2019.100722

Blum, R. W., & Libbey, H. P. (2004). School connectedness: Strengthening health and education outcomes for teenagers. *Journal of School Health*, 74(7), 229–299.

Breen, A. (2020). Back-to-school recommendations to boost students' and teachers' well-being. Retrieved October 17, 2020, from https://curry.virginia.edu/news/back-school-recommendations-boost-students%E2%80%99-and-teachers%E2%80%99-well-being

Broderick, P. C. (2019). *Mindfulness in the secondary classroom: A guide for teaching adolescents*. W. W. Norton & Company.

Brown, A. L., & Palincsar, A. S. (1989). Guided, cooperative learning and individual knowledge acquisition. In L. B. Resnick (Ed.), *Knowing, learning, and instruction: Essays in honor of Robert Glaser* (pp. 393–451). Lawrence Erlbaum Associates.

Brown, J. S. (1985). Idea-amplifiers: New kinds of electronic learning. *Educational Horizons*, 63, 108–112.

Brown, J. S., Collins, A., & Duguid, P. (1989). Situated cognition and the culture of learning. *Educational Researcher*, 18(1), 32–42. https://doi.org/10.3102/0013189X018001032

Center for Universal Design. (n.d.). *What is universal design: The 7 principles*. National Disability Authority. Retrieved August 15, 2020, http://universaldesign.ie/What-is-Universal-Design/The-7-Principles/

Chang, C.-C., Tseng, K.-H., Liang, C., & Liao, Y.-M. (2013). Constructing and evaluating online goal-setting mechanisms in web-based portfolio assessment system for facilitating self-regulated learning. *Computers & Education*, 69, 237–249. https://doi.org/10.1016/j.compedu.2013.07.016

Chappuis, S., & Stiggins, R. (2016). *Introduction to student-involved assessment FOR learning* (7th Ed.). Pearson.

Cho, M.-H., & Shen, D. (2013). Self-regulation in online learning. *Distance Education*, 34(3), 290–301. https://doi.org/10.1080/01587919.2013.835770

Cirillo, M., LaRochelle, R., Arbaugh, F., & Bieda, K. N. (2020). An innovative early field experience for preservice secondary teachers: Early results from shifting to an online model. *Journal of Technology and Teacher Education*, 28(2), 353–363. https://www.learntechlib.org/primary/p/216305/

Clark, R. E. (1983). Reconsidering research on learning from media. *Review of Educational Research*, 53(4), 445–459.

Collins, A., Brown, J. S., & Newman, S. E. (1987). *Cognitive apprenticeship: Teaching the craft of reading, writing and mathematics* (Technical Report No. 403). BBN Laboratories.

Cowan, N. (2001). The magical number 4 in short-term memory: A reconsideration of mental storage capacity. *Behavioral Brain Science, 24*(1), 87–114. https://doi.org/10.1017/s0140525x01003922

Cowan, N. (2010). The magical mystery four: How is working memory capacity limited, and why? *Current Directions in Psychological Science, 19*(1), 51–57.

Dawley, L., Rice, K., & Hinck, G. (2010). *Going Virtual! 2010: The status of professional development and unique needs of K-12 online teachers.* Boise State University.

Delen, E., & Liew, J. (2016). The use of interactive environments to promote self-regulation in online learning: A literature review. *European Journal of Contemporary Education, 15*(1), 24–33. https://doi.org/10.13187/ejced.2016.15.24

Dillenbourg, P. (1999). What do you mean by collaborative learning? In P. Dillenbourg (Ed.), *Collaborative learning: Cognitive and computational approaches* (pp. 1–19). Elsevier.

DiNucci, D. (1999). Fragmented future. *Print Magazine, 4*, 32. http://darcyd.com/fragmented_future.pdf

Dron, J., & Anderson, T. (2014). *Teaching crowds: Learning and social media.* AU Press. https://doi.org/10.15215/aupress/9781927356807.01

Duckworth, E. (2006). *"The having of wonderful ideas" and other essays on teaching and learning.* Teachers College.

Durlak, J. A., Weissberg, R. P., Dymnicki, A. B., Taylor, R. D., & Schellinger, K. B. (2011). The impact of enhancing students' social and emotional learning: A meta-analysis of school-based universal interventions. *Child Development, 82*(1), 405–432. https://doi.org/10.1111/j.1467-8624.2010.01564.x

Eisenberg, N. (Ed.). (2006). Social, emotional, and personality development. In W. Damon & R. M. Lerner (Eds.), *Handbook of child psychology* (6th ed., Vol. 3). Wiley.

Eshet-Alkalai, Y., & Soffer, O. (2012). Guest editorial—Navigating in the digital era: Digital literacy: Socio-cultural and educational aspects. *Educational Technology & Society, 15*(2), 1. https://go.gale.com/ps/anonymous?id=GALE%7CA2985037

62&sid=googleScholar&v=2.1&it=r&linkaccess=abs&issn=14364522&p=AONE&sw=w

Estes, T., & Mintz, S. (2016). *Instruction: A Models Approach*. Pearson Education.

Evergreen Education Group. (2020). *Snapshot 2020: A review of K–12 online, blended, and digital learning*. Retrieved August 28, 2020 from https://www.evergreenedgroup.com/s/DLC-KP-Snapshot2020-1.pdf

Ferrari, A. (2012). *Digital competence in practice: An analysis of frameworks*. European Commission. https://doi.org/10.2791/82116

Garrison, D. R., Anderson, T., & Archer, W. (2000). Critical inquiry in a text-based environment: Computer conferencing in higher education. *The Internet and Higher Education*, 2(2–3), 87–105.

Gibson, J. J. (1950). *The perception of the visible world*. Houghton Mifflin.

Gibson, J. J. (1966). *The senses considered as perceptual systems*. Houghton Mifflin.

Gokcearslan, S., & Alper, A. (2015). The effect of locus of control on learners' sense of community and academic success in the context of online learning communities. *The Internet and Higher Education*, 27, 64–73. https://doi.org/10.1016/j.iheduc.2015.06.003

Greenberg, M. T., Weissberg, R. P., O'Brien, M. U., Zins, J. E., Fredericks, L., Resnik, H., & Elias, M. J. (2003). Enhancing school-based prevention and youth development through coordinated social, emotional, and academic learning. *American Psychologist*, 58(6–7), 466–474. https://doi.org/10.1037/0003-066X.58.6-7.466

Guerra, N. G., & Bradshaw, C. P. (2008). Linking the prevention of problem behaviors and positive youth development: Core competencies for positive youth development and risk prevention. *New Directions in Child and Adolescent Development*, 122, 1–17. https://doi.org/10.1002/cd.225

Gunawardena, C. N., & McIsaac, M. S. (2004). Distance Education. In D. H. Jonassen (Ed.), *Handbook of Research on Educational Communications and Technology* (2nd ed., pp. 355–396). Lawrence Erlbaum Associates.

Gunawardena, C. N., Frechette, C., & Layne, L. (2019). *Culturally inclusive instructional design: A framework and guide to building online wisdom communities*. Routledge.

Gunawardena, C. N., & Zittle, F. J. (1997). Social presence as a predictor of satisfaction within a computer-mediated conferencing environment. *American Journal of Distance Education, 11*(3), 8–26. https://doi.org/10.1080/08923649709526970

Hartshorne, R., Baumgartner, E., Kaplan-Rakowski, R., Mouza, C., & Ferdig, R. E. (2020). Special issue editorial: Preservice and inservice professional development during the COVID-19 pandemic. *Journal of Technology and Teacher Education, 28*(2), 137–147. https://www.learntechlib.org/primary/p/216910/

Headleand, C. (2020, September 8). Pastoral care in the blended classroom. *Chris Headleand.* https://chrisheadleand.com/2020/09/08/pastoral-care-in-the-blended-classroom/

Hodges, C., Moore, S., Lockee, B., Bond, A., & Jewett, A. (2021). An Instructional Design Process for Emergency Remote Teaching. In A. Tlili, D. Burgos, & A. Tabacco (Eds.) *Education in crisis context: COVID-19 as an opportunity for global learning.* Springer.

Hodges, C., Moore, S., Lockee, B., Trust, T., & Bond, A. (2020, March 27). The difference between emergency remote teaching and online learning. *EDUCAUSE Review.* Retrieved September 12, 2020 from https://er.educause.edu/articles/2020/3/the-difference-between-emergency-remote-teaching-and-online-learning

Jain, S., Bassey, H., Brown, M. A., & Kalra, P. (2014). *Restorative justice in Oakland schools: Implementation and impacts.* Oakland Unified School District. https://www.ousd.org/cms/lib07/CA01001176/Centricity/Domain/134/OUSD-RJ%20Report%20revised%20Final.pdf

Jekielek, S. M., Moore, K. A., Hair, E. C., & Scarupa, H. J. (2002). *Mentoring: A promising strategy for youth development* [Research Brief]. Child Trends.

Jennings, P. A. (2019). *Mindfulness in the PreK-5 classroom: Evidence-based tips and tools to stress less and learn more.* W. W. Norton & Company.

Jensen, L. & Deemer, E. (2019). Identity, campus climate, and burnout among undergraduate women in STEM fields. *The Career Development Quarterly, 67*(2), 96–109.

Joo, Y. J., Lim, K. Y., & Kim, J. (2013). Locus of control, self-efficacy, and task value as predictors of learning outcome in an online university context. *Computers & Education, 62*, 149–158. https://doi.org/10.1016/j.compedu.2012.10.027

Kennedy, K., & Archambault, L. (2012). Offering preservice teachers field experiences in K-12 online learning: A national survey of teacher education programs. *Journal of Teacher Education, 63*(3), 185–200. https://doi.org/10.1177/0022487111433651

Kennedy, K., & Ferdig, R. E. (Eds.). (2018). *Handbook of Research of K12 Online and Blended Learning (2nd ed.)*. ETC Press. Retrieved August 28, 2020, from https://www.learntechlib.org/p/182993/

Kier, M., & Clark, K. (2020). The rapid response of William & Mary's School of Education to support preservice teachers and equitably provide mentoring to elementary learners in a culture of an international pandemic. *Journal of Technology and Teacher Education, 28*(2), 321–327. https://www.learntechlib.org/primary/p/216153/

Kirschner, P. A., & van Merriënboer, J. J. G. (2013). Do learners really know best? Urban legends in education. *Educational Psychologist, 48*(3), 169–183.

Kreijns, K., Kirschner, P. A., Jochems, W., & van Buuren, H. (2011). Measuring perceived social presence in distributed learning groups. *Education and Information Technologies, 16*, 365–381. https://doi.org/10.1007/s10639-010-9135-7

Lang, J. (2013). *Cheating lessons: Learning from academic dishonesty*. Harvard University Press.

Lave, J. (1990). The culture of acquisition and the practice of understanding. In J. Stigler, R. Schweder, & G. Herdt (Eds.), *Cultural Psychology: Essays on Comparative Human Development* (pp. 309–327). Cambridge University Press. doi:10.1017/CBO9781139173728.010Lin, J.-W., Lai, Y.-C., Lai, Y.-C., & Chang, L.-C. (2016). Fostering self-regulated learning in a blended environment using group awareness and peer assistance as external scaffolds. *Journal of Computer Assisted Learning, 32*(1), 77–93. https://doi.org/10.1111/jcal.12120

Lipman, M. (1991). *Thinking in education*. Cambridge University Press.

Lynch, R., & Dembo, M. (2004). The Relationship Between Self-Regulation and Online Learning in a Blended Learning Context. *The International Review of Research in Open and Distributed Learning, 5*(2). https://doi.org/10.19173/irrodl.v5i2.189

Maddux, C. D. (2001). Solving accessibility and other problems in school and classroom web sites. *Rural Special Education Quarterly, 20*(4), 11–18. https://doi.org/10.1177/875687050102000403

Masten, A. S., & Coatsworth, J. D. (1998). The development of competence in favorable and unfavorable environments: Lessons from research on successful children. *American Psychologist, 53*(2), 205–220. https://doi.org/10.1037/0003-066X.53.2.205

Means, B., Bakia, M., & Murphy, R. (2014). *Learning online: What research tells us about whether, when and how.* Routledge.

Meyer, A., Rose, D., & Gordon, D. (2014). *Universal design for learning: Theory and practice.* CAST.

Molseed, T. (2011). An analysis of peer review response types in threaded discussions of an online graduate class. *American Journal of Distance Education, 25*(4), 254–267.

Moore, M. G. (1989). Editorial: Three types of interaction. *The American Journal of Distance Education, 3*(2), 1–7. https://doi.org/10.1080/08923648909526659

Moore, M. G. (1990). Recent contributions to the theory of distance education. *Open Learning, 5*(3), 10–15.

Moore, M. G. (1993). Theory of transactional distance. In D. Keegan (Ed.), *Theoretical principles of distance education* (pp. 22–38). Routledge.

Moore, M. G., & Kearsley, G. (2012). *Distance education: A systematic view of online learning* (3rd ed.). Wadsworth Cengage Learning.

Moore, S. L. (2020). *Designing Interactive Online Courses—Quick Reference Guide.* Norton.

Moore, S., & Hoffman, A. (2020, November 6). *An analysis of school division needs on new teacher induction.* Association for Educational Communications and Technology, virtual conference.

Morrison, G. R., Ross, S. M., Morrison, J. R., & Kalman, H. K. (2019). *Designing effective instruction* (8th ed.). Wiley.

National Research Council. (2000). *How people learn: Brain, mind, experience, and school: Expanded edition.* National Academies Press.

Ng, C. (2012). The role of self-efficacy, control beliefs and achievement goals on learning among distance learners. In J. L. Moore & A. D. Benson, *International perspectives of distance learning in higher education* (pp. 233–252). InTech.

Norman, D. (2013). *The design of everyday things: Revised and expanded edition.* Basic Books.

Oh, E., & Reeves, T. C. (2014). Generational differences and the integration of technology in learning, instruction, and performance. In J. Spector, M. Merrill, J. Elen, & M. Bishop (Eds.), *Handbook of Research on Educational Communications and Technology*. Springer. https://doi.org/10.1007/978-1-4614-3185-5_66

Oviatt, S. (2006). Human-centered design meets cognitive load theory: Designing interfaces that help people think. In *Proceedings of the 14th ACM international conference on Multimedia* (pp. 871–880). Association for Computing Machinery. https://doi.org/10.1145/1180639.1180831

Pardales, M. & Girod, M. (2013). Community of inquiry: Its past and present future. *Educational Philosophy and Theory, 38*(3), 299–309.

Park, E. [@MrsParkShine]. (n.d.). *I made breakout room choice doors where Ss will "go" to during their work time. We're using Google Meet . . .* [Tweet; includes image]. Twitter. Retrieved August 31, 2020, from https://twitter.com/MrsParkShine/status/1300401054404796416?s=20

Parker, J. & Herrington, J. (2015). Setting the climate in an authentic online community of learning. *Australian Association for Research in Education*, Paper presented at the Annual Meeting of the Australian Association for Research in Education (AARE) (Freemantle, Western Australia, Nov 29-Dec 3, 2015).

Porat, E., Blau, I., & Barak, A. (2018). Measuring digital literacies: Junior high-school students' perceived competencies versus actual performance. *Computers & Education, 126*, 23–36. https://doi.org/10.1016/j.compedu.2018.06.030

Poropat, A. E. (2009). A meta-analysis of the five-factor model of personality and academic performance. *Psychological Bulletin, 135*(2), 322–338. https://psycnet.apa.org/fulltext/2009-02580-011.html

Quinn, C. (2018). *Millennials, goldfish & other training misconceptions: Debunking learning myths and misconceptions*. Association for Talent Development (ATD).

Resnick, L. B. (1991). Shared cognition: Thinking as social practice. In L. B. Resnick, J. M. Levine, & S. D. Teasley (Eds.), *Perspectives on socially shared cognition* (pp. 1–20). American Psychological Association. https://doi.org/10.1037/10096-018

Richardson, J. C., Maeda, Y., Lv, J., & Caskurlu, S. (2017). Social presence in relation to students' satisfaction and learning in the online environment: A meta-analysis. *Computers in Human Behavior, 71*, 402–417.

Richardson, J. C., & Swan, K. (2003). Examining social presence in online courses in relation to students' perceived learning and satisfaction. *Journal of Asynchronous Learning Networks, 7*(1), 68–88. https://www.ideals.illinois.edu/handle/2142/18713

Richardson, M., Abraham, C., & Bond, R. (2012). Psychological correlates of university students' academic performance: A systematic review and meta-analysis. *Psychological Bulletin, 138*(2), 353–387. https://doi.org/10.1037/a0026838

Rienties, B., & Toetenel, L. (2016). The impact of learning design on student behaviour, satisfaction and performance: A cross-institutional comparison across 151 modules. *Computers in Human Behavior, 60,* 333–341. https://doi.org/10.1016/j.chb.2016.02.074

Rothbart, M.K. (2007). Temperament, development, and personality. *Current Directions in Psychological Science, 16* (4), 207–212.

Rovai, A. (2007). Facilitating online discussions effectively. *The Internet and Higher Education, 10*(1), 77–88. https://doi.org/10.1016/j.iheduc.2006.10.001

Rummler, G., & Brache, A. (1995). *Improving performance: How to manage the white space in the organization chart.* Jossey-Bass.

Russell, T. L. (2001). *The No Significant Difference Phenomenon.* IDECC.

Rutherford, T. [@DrTeyaR]. (n.d.). *Did a quick padlet activity in class yesterday. I especially like the "color code notes" response on an activity . . .* [Tweet; includes image]. Twitter. Retrieved September 11, 2020 from https://twitter.com/DrTeyaR/status/1304419052958486529?s=20.

Saklofske, D. H., Austin, E. J., Mastoras, S. M., Beaton, L., & Osborne, S. E. (2012). Relationships of personality, affect, emotional intelligence and coping with student stress and academic success: Different patterns of association for stress and success. *Learning and Individual Differences, 22*(2), 251–257. https://doi.org/10.1016/j.lindif.2011.02.010

Schlatter, T., & Levinson, D. (2013). *Visual usability: Principles and practices for designing digital applications.* Elsevier.

Schön, D. (1967). *Technology and change: The new Heraclitus.* Oxford.

Schön, D. (2017). *The reflective practitioner: How professionals think in action.* Taylor & Francis. (Original work published 1983)

Short, J., Williams, E., & Christie, B. (1976). *The social psychology of telecommunications*. Wiley.

Srinivasan, M. (2019). *SEL every day: Integrating social and emotional learning with instruction in secondary classrooms*. W. W. Norton & Company.

Stiggins, R. J., & Conklin, N. F. (1992). *In teachers' hands: Investigating the practices of classroom assessment*. State University of New York Press.

Swauger, S. (2020). Our bodies encoded: Algorithmic test proctoring in higher education. In J. Stommel, C. Friend, & S. M. Morris (Eds.), *Critical digital pedagogy: A collection*. Hybrid Pedagogy.

Tsai, C.-C., Chuang, S.-C., Liang, J.-C., & Tsai, M.-J. (2011). Self-efficacy in internet-based learning environments: A literature review. *Journal of Educational Technology & Society, 14*(4), 222–240. https://www.jstor.org/stable/10.2307/jeductechsoci.14.4.222

Triner, D., Greenberry, A., & Watkins, R. (1996). Training needs assessment: A contradiction in terms? *Educational Technology, 36*(6), 51–55.

Tu, C.-H. (2001). How Chinese perceive social presence: An examination of interaction in online learning environment. *Educational Media International, 38*(1), 45–60. https://doi.org/10.1080/09523980010021235

U.S. Department of Education. (2010). *Evaluation of evidence-based practices in online learning: A meta-analysis and review of online learning studies.* https://www2.ed.gov/rschstat/eval/tech/evidence-based-practices/finalreport.pdf

VanLehn, K., & Brown, J. S. (1980). Planning nets: A representation for formalizing analogies and semantic models for procedural skills. In R. E. Snow, P. A. Federico, & W. E. Montague (Eds.), *Aptitude Learning and Instruction: Vol. 2: Cognitive Process Analyses of Learning and Problem-Solving*. Erlbaum.

Vedel, A. (2014). The Big Five and tertiary academic performance: A systematic review and meta-analysis. *Personality and Individual Differences, 71*, 66–76. https://doi.org/10.1016/j.paid.2014.07.011

Virginia Department of Education. (2020). *Recover, redesign, restart: A comprehensive plan that moves Virginia learners and educators forward.* Retrieved October 15, 2020 from http://www.doe.virginia.gov/support/health_medical/covid-19/recover-redesign-restart-2020.pdf

Wang, A. Y., & Newlin, M. H. (2000). Characteristics of students who enroll and succeed in psychology Web-based classes. *Journal of Educational Psychology, 92*(1), 137–143. https://doi.org/10.1037/0022-0663.92.1.137

Watkins, R. (2007). *Performance by design: The systematic selection, design, and development of performance technologies that produce useful results.* HRD Press.

Weissberg, R. P., & Greenberg, M. T. (1998). School and community competence-enhancement and prevention programs. In W. Damon, I. E. Sigel, & K. A. Renninger (Eds.), *Handbook of child psychology: Child psychology in practice* (pp. 877–954). John Wiley & Sons.

White, B. Y. (1984). Designing computer games to help physics students understand Newton's laws of motion. *Cognition and Instruction, 1,* 69–108.

Whiteside, A. L., & Garrett Dikkers, A. (2012). Maximizing multicultural online learning experiences with the Social Presence Model, course examples, and specific strategies. In K. St. Amant & S. Kelsey (Eds.), *Computer-mediated communication across cultures: International interactions in online environments* (pp. 395–413). IGI Global.

Wiggins, G., & McTighe, J. (2005). *Understanding by design* (2nd ed.). Association for Supervision and Curriculum Development.

Wladis, C., & Samuels, J. (2016). Do online readiness surveys do what they claim? Validity, reliability, and subsequent student enrollment decisions. *Computers & Education, 98,* 39–56. https://doi.org/10.1016/j.compedu.2016.03.001

Yoder, N. (2014). *Teaching the whole child: Instructional practices that support social-emotional learning in three teacher evaluation frameworks.* American Institutes for Research.

Yukselturk, E., & Bulut, S. (2007). Predictors for student success in an online course. *Journal of Educational Technology & Society, 10*(2), 71–83. https://www.jstor.org/stable/10.2307/jeductechsoci.10.2.71

Zhao, Y., Lei, J., Yan, B., Lai, C., & Tan, H. (2005). What makes the difference? A practical analysis of research on the effectiveness of distance education. *The Teachers College Record, 107,* 1836–1884.

Zimmerman, B. J. (1989). A social cognitive view of self-regulated academic learning. *Journal of Educational Psychology, 81*(3), 329–339. https://doi.org/10.1037/0022-0663.81.3.329

Zimmerman, B. J. (2002). Becoming a self-regulated learner: An overview. *Theory into Practice, 41*(2), 64–70. https://doi.org/10.1207/s15430421tip4102_2

Zimmerman, B. J., & Schunk, D. H. (2011). Self-regulated learning and performance: An introduction and an overview. In B. J. Zimmerman & D. H. Schunk (Eds.), *Handbook of self-regulation of learning and performance* (pp. 1–12). Routledge.

Index

About the Author

Stephanie L. Moore is Assistant Professor of Organization, Information, and Learning Sciences at the University of New Mexico. Her areas of expertise include online and blended learning, multimedia learning, ethics of educational technologies, and accessibility and UDL. She has designed and taught online for over 20 years. Prior to joining UNM, she taught at the University of Virginia, including designing a class on online learning for teachers that featured a virtual practicum. Across her career, she has helped to build and lead effective online learning solutions that have won multiple awards such as the AACTE Innovation of the Year Award.